English

ISEB
Independent Schools
Examinations Board

13+

for
Common Entrance

Study and Revision Guide

KORNEL KOSSUTH

HODDER
EDUCATION
AN HACHETTE UK COMPANY

The publisher would like to thank the following for permission to reproduce copyright material:

Acknowledgments:

p14 extract from 'Church Going' by Philip Larkin from *Collected Poems*, edited by Anthony Thwaite (© The Marvell Press and Faber & Faber, 1988); **p26** extract from *Life of Pi* by Yann Martel (© Canongate Books, 2002); **p28** extract from *The Bafut Beagles* by Gerard Durrell (© Penguin Books, 1958); **p30** extract from *Boy* by Roald Dahl (© Jonathan Cape, 1984); **p32** extract from Act One, Scene One from *A.D. A Trilogy of Plays* by Edwin Morgan (Carcanet Press, 2000), reproduced by permission of Carcanet Press Ltd; **p34&35** 'Of John Davidson' from *Complete Poems, Volume 1*, edited by Michael Grieve (Carcanet Press, 1993), reproduced by permission of Carcanet Press Ltd; **p36** extract from 'Manjimup' by Charles Causley from *Collected Poems 1951–2000* (© Picador, 2000), reproduced by permission of David Higham; **p37** 'Blessing' from *Postcards from god* by Imtiaz Dharker (Bloodaxe Books, 1997), reproduced by permission of the publisher; **p38** 'The Road Not Taken' from *The Poetry of Robert Frost*, edited by Edward Connery Lathem (© Jonathan Cape, 1969); **p41** lines from 'Night Mail, III' by W H Auden from *Collected Shorter Poems 1927–1957* (© Faber & Faber, 1969); **p43** extract from 'Colonel Fazackerley' by Charles Causley from *Collected Poems for Children* (© Macmillan Children's Books, 2000), reproduced by permission of David Higham; **p44** extract from 'If You Should Go to Caistor Town' by Charles Causley from *Collected Poems 1951–2000* (© Picador, 2000), reproduced by permission of David Higham, 'Sonnet XLIII' by Edna St. Vincent Millay from *Vanity Fair* (November, 1920); **p45** '585: I like to see it lap the Miles-' by Emily Dickinson from *Poems, Second Series* (1891); **p47** 'Twelve Songs, XI' by W H Auden from *Collected Shorter Poems 1927–1957* (© Faber & Faber, 1969); **p91** extract from *The Peregrine* by J A Baker (© HarperCollins, 2011); **p95** : 'Cynddylan on a Tractor' from *Collected Poems 1945–1990* (Phoenix, 2000), © R S Thomas 1993; **p107** extract from 'Strange Meeting' from *The Collected Poems of Wilfred Owen* (Chatto & Windus, 1963), © The Executors of Harold Owen's Estate 1920, 1931, 1963

The publishers have made every effort to secure permission to reprint material protected by copyright. They will be pleased to make good any omissions brought to their attention in future printings of this book.

Photo credits:
p 38 © The Art Gallery Collection/Alamy

Although every effort has been made to ensure that website addresses are correct at time of going to press, Hodder Education cannot be held responsible for the content of any website mentioned. It is sometimes possible to find a relocated web page by typing in the address of the home page for a website in the URL window of your browser.

Orders: please contact Bookpoint Ltd, 130 Milton Park, Abingdon, Oxon OX14 4SB. Telephone: (44) 01235 827720. Fax: (44) 01235 400454. Lines are open 9.00–17.00, Monday to Saturday, with a 24-hour message answering service. Visit our website at www.hoddereducation.co.uk

© Kornel Kossuth 2013

First published in 2013 by
Hodder Education
An Hachette UK Company,
Carmelite House, 50 Victoria Embankment,
London EC4Y 0DZ

Impression number   5   4   3

Year   2017   2016

Cover photo © selenamay – Fotolia.com
Illustrations by Datapage (India) Pvt. Ltd.

Typeset in Bembo Std 12 pts by Datapage (India) Pvt. Ltd.
Printed in India

A catalogue record for this title is available from the British Library

ISBN 978 1 444 19962 8

Contents

6 Paper 2 Section B: Creative writing

7 In the exam

8 Practice paper ...89

Appendix

Glossary ...105

Introduction

Welcome to this Study and Revision Guide. Inside the covers of this book you will find all the information you need to succeed in the ISEB 13+ English Common Entrance examination. This does not mean that this book has just made your teacher redundant. It hasn't. Nothing beats direct contact with a good teacher when you want to learn. But if you work through this book carefully as a reminder and stimulant, then you will have all the tools you need to do well in CE.

The idea for this guide came to me when a number of pupils I was teaching struggled to grasp how to answer comprehension questions correctly. The revision guides available only showed what a good answer might look like, but gave scant guidance on how to get to such an answer. This was intensely frustrating for the pupils and for me as their teacher. So I set about remedying the situation and writing this guide, the tenets of which I have tested through many years of teaching. It works.

The idea of this guide is therefore simple: in each part it will show you how to get to good answers that gain high marks. The emphasis throughout is on practicality and doing it yourself. This is easier to do with comprehension questions, where the answers are slightly more limited and predictable. With the writing tasks, most of the DIY will involve you going out and writing. There are mark grids included to help you work out how well you did and where you need to improve.

The order of the parts in this book does not follow that of the CE papers, but groups the comprehension exercises together and then the writing tasks together. There is, at the end of the book, a full mock CE paper so that you know what a paper looks like and in which order the sections are presented.

Although primarily addressed to pupils, this guide can equally be used by teachers to support class work to revise for CE or by parents to help their children in the run-up to those final exams.

I hope you find this guide as useful as my pupils have in the past. If you have any suggestions, let me know and I hope to be able to incorporate them in a subsequent edition.

Kornel Kossuth

September 2013

1 Section A: Comprehensions

The information in this part applies to Section A of both Paper 1 and Paper 2. These sections have a lot in common: in particular, the kind of questions they ask, and the way you should deal with these questions. The main difference lies in the type of text used.

The reading section

Section A of each paper contains written comprehension questions on a given text. Each reading section carries the same number of marks (25).

In Detail

The comprehensions will test your skill at:

- reading between the lines of text and finding out things that are not necessarily stated in the text, but that can be found out from it
- arguing points of view on the basis of the text
- knowing how authors write and how they make their writing more effective.

So, the comprehension exercise is less about recalling information from the passage and more about its effect and how this effect is achieved. Sometimes the questions will also ask you for some form of personal reaction to the passage.

Questions usually carry 1 to 6 (sometimes 8 or even 10) marks.

You have 1 hour 15 minutes to complete each paper, so roughly 35 to 40 minutes for each Section A.

Key terms

Literary means that the passage is well written, making use of a number of literary techniques.

Prose is what you normally write: ordinary written language without a set rhythm pattern – basically everything except poetry.

Paper 1: Section A

This section contains a literary prose passage of roughly one A4 sheet in length (or longer) and about five or six questions on the passage. The piece can be taken from a novel, a short story, a play, travel writing or an (auto)biography.

Paper 2: Section A

This section contains a poem, usually by a twentieth-century poet, and, again, five or six questions on the poem. Examiners try to choose poetry that deals with things you will be familiar with.

The texts

In each section you will be given a text, also called a passage or extract. The prose text (in Section A) will usually be taken from a longer piece of writing. The introduction to the passage will set the scene or provide important background information so that you understand the passage. The poem, however, is normally complete and not taken out of a longer poem. If it is, this will be explained in the introduction to the text or to the questions.

Make sure you read all the introductions and look closely at the information on the texts (usually given at the end of the text or the paper).

(Total marks: 50)

The prose passage entitled *There's Always One,* from *The Learning Game* by Jonathan Smith, is published by Little Brown and Company.

The poem is *Driving to Switzerland* by Anthony Wilson, published in *Nowhere Better Than This* by Worple Press 2002.

This will help you to find out whether the author is male or female and may also give you an idea of when the passages were written. Remember, as recently as twenty years ago a lot of the things that you take for granted may not have been quite so common – or even around at all! Think, for example, about the internet, mobile phones and other gadgets that we use every day.

Read the passages as thoroughly as possible, taking in as much as you can of what is mentioned where, what images the text contains and any other points you may find of interest. The idea is not to read the text as quickly as possible, but to read it as closely as possible, so you have a good working knowledge and understanding of it. The more carefully you read the text, the more easily you will find information in it and the more likely you are to understand it and how it functions.

> **Examiner's tip**
>
> Feel free to make any notes or markings on the paper itself that might help you to find certain passages again.

In Detail

Who is who?

the author the person who wrote the extract

the writer the same as the author

the poet the author of the poem (Paper 2 Section A). The author of the extract in Paper 1 can never be called a poet.

the narrator the person telling the story; here the story is usually told in the first person singular ('I'). You should not assume that the narrator is the author, unless the text is from an autobiography.

Never refer to authors by their first name. Use either their surname or whole name. So:

Anthony Wilson wrote the poem 'Driving to Switzerland'. In it Wilson tells of a journey he had as a young boy.

(Do *not* use 'Anthony'!)

Types of questions

The questions you will be asked can be grouped into four basic types. Knowing which type of question you are being asked will help you to know how to deal with it.

Question type	Marks	How to answer
RECALL Find and write down information from the text, either quoted or in your own words.	Usually 1, 2 or 3	Make as many points, or find as many quotations, as there are marks. There is no need to quote from the text, unless this is specified – you may have to use your own words!

Examples of recall

What are the three things the author mentions as being the most important discoveries of the fifteenth century?

Write in your own words two reasons the author gives for wanting to ban obese people from flying.

What three verbs does the author use to describe the way the boy is running?

Examiner's tip

This is usually the introductory question and is not designed to be hard.

Question type	Marks	How to answer
TECHNIQUE Explain or discuss the effectiveness of the language using quotes or references to the text.	Usually an even number of marks	Name and explain (or discuss) one technique from the text for every 2 marks. For example, for 4 marks, PEEL twice: name and explain (or discuss) two techniques, using quotes. See page 11 for further information on PEEL-ing.

Examples of technique

How does the author make the description of the march through the mountains effective?

How does the author use sight and sound to bring to life the cities of Judah?

In what way does the author bring out the humour of the car stopping in the middle of nowhere?

Examiner's tip

Here the main object is to explain how language is used effectively in the text.

Note

If the question has an odd number of marks, then you should either make the same number of short points as there are marks or write a more extended answer. For an extended answer, treat the question as if it were worth 1 mark more, so for example provide three PEELs for a 5-mark question.

Question type	Marks	How to answer
THOUGHT Describe, explain or argue something and refer to the text or use quotations to support your point.	Usually an even number of marks	Describe, explain or argue one point for every 2 marks and use one quotation *for each of these points*. For example, for 8 marks, PEEL four times: argue four points and use one quotation for each of these arguments. See page 11 for further information on PEEL-ing.

Examples of thought

What impression do you get of the general from this extract?

Do you think the author enjoys her experience? Give reasons for your answer.

Do you think the boy will be successful in trying to persuade his father to let him play on the bomb-site? Explain your reasons and refer to the text closely in your answer.

Examiner's tip

Here the main object is to argue a case and use the text to support your point of view or to infer something from the text. Thought questions often ask about character.

Note

As with the technique questions, if a thought question has an odd number of marks, then you should make that number of short points or write a more extended answer.

Question type	Marks	How to answer
RESPONSE Give your own opinion or response to the text.	4, 5 or 6 marks	Here marks are awarded depending on how well the text is used and referred to in the answer as well as how clearly points are made and argued.

Examples of responce

Would you like to go on a holiday with the author's family? Give reasons for your answer.

Have you had a similar experience to the author's? Describe it and say in what way it relates to the passage.

Imagine you are a member of the parliament to whom this speech is addressed. How would you react?

Examiner's tip

This is usually the last question and tests how well you have understood the text as a whole and whether you can relate it to your own experience.

PEEL-ing

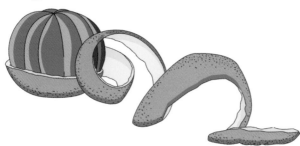

Technique and thought questions both (usually) require you to PEEL. PEEL-ing is a technique that allows you to make a point and explain your thoughts in a structured way. It helps you to know what to say and when to stop saying it.

PEEL stands for:

P-oint   This is stating your argument or naming the technique the author is using; basically answering the question very briefly.

E-vidence   The evidence for your point is either a reference to the passage or a quotation.

E-xplain   Here you explain your argument in detail or analyse the quotation in detail. Try to be as precise as possible.

L-ink   At the end you reinforce your point, thus linking your arguments back to the beginning. In most comprehension exercises you can leave this out if pressed for time.

The most important parts of a PEEL are the evidence and the explanation.

The point needs to be short and clear and the evidence – the quotation or reference to the excerpt – should be only the words that you need to make your point.

When you are in the exam (or doing a practice paper) and are confronted with a question that requires you to PEEL, you should first of all select the quotation you want to use.

Examiner's tip

When choosing the quotation, remember there is no right or wrong answer. You can use any piece of evidence, as long as you can explain *why* the phrase you have selected is relevant to the question.

Technique question	Thought question
Find the quotation you want to use (whichever words strike you as being particularly effective).	Find the quotation you want to use (whichever words strike you as showing what you are being asked to explain).
Name the technique.	Think about what point you can infer from the quotation (e.g. which characteristic does it show?).
Start writing your PEEL, beginning with the name of the technique (as above) and then your quotation (copied correctly).	Start writing your PEEL, beginning with the point you are making (as above) and then your quotation (copied correctly).
Make sure you explain the effectiveness of the technique, focusing on the word that is the most important or striking.	State how your quotation supports the point, making sure to use common sense and making a clear link from the quotation to the point.

There can be some overlap between the various types of questions, especially between response and thought questions. Thought questions use the text more closely and ask you to analyse it, to infer information from the text; response questions ask you to be somehow involved in the text, to interact with it or imagine yourself in it. While you may use quotations in a response question, you will not be PEEL-ing.

Other types of questions that you may come across include those:

■ asking you for a definition of a certain technique (e.g. What is alliteration?)
■ testing your knowledge of words (e.g. What does docile (line 4) mean?)
■ asking you to summarise parts of the passage – essentially a recall question, but more long-winded (e.g. 'Summarise in your own words the author's point of view in the third paragraph').

Recognising the type of question can be difficult at first, but practice – as well as a careful reading of what the question is asking you – will make you perfect.

Signal words

Certain question types often have the same word or phrase in them. Here are the most frequent of these signals:

Recall: 'in your own words' (if you are being asked to put something in your own words, you often only have to find that something)

Technique: 'how does the author/poet/writer', 'effect', 'effective', 'effectiveness', 'vivid'

Thought: 'what impression', 'do you think'

Signal words are not foolproof, but they can give a strong indication of the type of question you may be dealing with.

Test yourself

Try the following exercise. All you have to do is identify the question type (recall, technique, thought, response). This may not always be clear because you do not have the marks or the text in front of you, but you should be able to narrow each question down to two possible types.

1 How does the author make the hunt come to life?
2 Would you like to have a sister like Eleanor?
3 In your own words, state what the two greatest risks facing skiers are.
4 Explain why the author disapproves of cars.
5 What kind of a person is the uncle? You should refer to the text in your answer.
6 What do we learn about the family in the first paragraph?
7 Using your own words, explain why schools no longer have fields for games.
8 In what way does the author make the journey sound tense?

Test yourself

How should you answer the following questions?

For example, 'Is murder a good topic for a poem?' (5 marks). This is a response question, as it is asking for a more general reaction to the poem, rather than analysis of the text. Here the marks are not directly related to what you write. You should try and write as best you can, using quotations where applicable.

1 How does the author make it clear that Sam is exerting himself?   (6 marks)
2 What things is the narrator most afraid of?   (2 marks)
3 Do you think the trapper will catch the fox? Refer closely to the text in your answer.   (4 marks)
4 What is the point the poet is trying to make in this poem?   (5 marks)
5 How do you prepare for the coming of winter? You can use ideas from the poem in your answer. (4 marks)
6 The author uses humour a lot in this extract. Find three instances of this and explain carefully
   in each case how the humour is effective.   (9 marks)
7 What kind of a person do you think the narrator is?   (5 marks)
8 What four things happen regularly in Colorado?   (2 marks)

How to answer the questions

Quoting from the text

When you quote from the text make sure the quotation fits the question and use as short a quotation as possible. It is best if you can make it part of what you write. When quoting from a poem, do not just quote a line, but quote units of sense. If you are quoting more than one line from a poem, use a slash '/' to denote a line break. Remember to keep all capital letters as in the original.

For example, look at the first five lines of Philip Larkin's poem 'Church Going':

> Once I am sure there's nothing going on
> I step inside, letting the door thud shut.
> Another church: matting, seats, and stone,
> And little books; sprawlings of flowers, cut
> For Sunday, brownish now;

An example of a short quotation integrated into the text would be:

> In the poem, the narrator lets the church door 'thud shut', emphasising the large hollow emptiness of the room inside.

An example of a quotation of more than one line would be:

> The poem has an air of melancholy decay, made clear when it says 'flowers, cut / For Sunday, brownish now'.

Do not make any mistakes when quoting from the text – it is extremely careless.

Recall questions

Answering a recall question usually just involves writing down the word(s) from the passage that you have been asked to find. If the question asks you to put it in your own words, do *not* use quotations or the words used in the text. Use different words that mean the same thing.

For example:

> a programme of raising funds by selling off school playing fields

could become:

> schools tried to increase their available money by selling their games pitches.

Test yourself (Recall)

Read the following passage and then answer the questions that follow it.

Nowadays a person cannot be said to be hip unless they have a whole range of electronic gadgetry, a facebook and twitter account as well as a lack of shame. The veritable explosion of slim, white tablets, pads, pods, pids, invariably preceded by the letter 'i', is more than matched by the frenzy which accompanies each new product. That people are willing to queue a whole night long for a flashy design, when you can have just as good without queuing and admittedly without the design, says a lot about our culture. We have all become designed shop fronts, peddling our personal lives in little chunks that easily stick in the throat.

1 In your own words, state what a person nowadays has to have or do to be cool and modern. (3)
2 How are the various gadgets described in the text? (2)
3 In your own words, describe what people are prepared to queue for. (1)
4 What does the author say we have all become? (1)
5 State, in your own words, what the author thinks says a lot about our culture. (2)

Technique questions

These types of questions ask you how the author creates an effect or achieves a certain mood or atmosphere. They are therefore asking you about how the author uses language and the effect the language has, *not* about what the author is saying. Therefore, as a rule, do *not* just repeat passages from the text.

There are a number of techniques that an author may use. The glossary at the end of this book explains many of these techniques in more detail, with examples. The most important ones to know and recognise are: simile, metaphor, personification, symbol, irony, onomatopoeia, alliteration, assonance and tricolon as well as rhyme, rhythm and metre.

Remember to explain the *effect* these techniques have (see below).

Remember – if asked – you must provide evidence from the text (either a quotation or a reference) *for each technique you mention*.

Examiner's tip

Sometimes you may come across a phrase which you find particularly evocative, but you may not be able to identify the technique. In these cases, there are two phrases you can usually use: 'describing detail' or 'powerful words'.

How to analyse the effectiveness of language

Rather than state that language is effective because it 'makes the reader see or imagine the scene' (which is not saying anything, really), look at the words and explain how they work in the context.

A useful technique to help you do this, especially when dealing with imagery, is to explain what the words usually mean, what mood or atmosphere they evoke, and then to relate that to the passage you have read.

1 Find which words are the important or unusual ones (which words 'carry the weight') – you don't have to write this down, just be clear about it in your head.
2 Explain what these words usually mean, in everyday life.
3 Explain what these words therefore mean in the context of the passage – how they enrich our understanding.

For example, an analysis of the simile 'The spaghetti looked like a nest of worms' could be broken down as follows:

The unusual or important part of the simile is the 'nest of worms'.

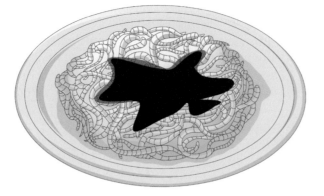

'nest of worms' *Usual meaning*	'nest of worms' *In the passage*
worm: a long, slimy and squirmy, earth-dwelling animal nest: a dense, interwoven pile or heap of twigs and leaves	Because the spaghetti are long and thin, they look like worms, a comparison suggested by the fact that they are covered in brownish tomato sauce. They are piled high, like a nest, but seem to writhe and be alive, underlining the gruesome and unsavoury nature of the meal.

The whole analysis would read something like this:

Worms are long, slimy, squirming animals and a nest is a dense pile of twigs. By saying the spaghetti – long and thin noodles covered in brownish tomato sauce – look like worms, which are similar in shape and colour and texture, the author is underlining the gruesome nature of this meal as no one would want to eat live worms. This effect is heightened by the fact that it is a nest of worms, so a whole pile that seems to be writhing and alive; a more than unsavoury meal.

Sound effects

When trying to explain the effectiveness of sound effects, you should go into the details of the sounds being used. This will involve referring to hard and sudden (or explosive) sounds like 'p' or 't' or soft sounds like 's' or 'oo'.

Make sure that you write about phonics – the sounds of letters – rather than the letters (or their names). For example, the letter combinations 'ti', 'sh', 'ssi', 'ci' and 'ch' all (can) produce the sound 'sh' as in nation, shun, passion, magician and chef respectively. For all these, you can refer to the 'sh-sound'.

An analysis of the word 'battered' as onomatopoeia might read as follows:

> The explosive 'b' sound at the beginning gives the impression of a blunt object hitting something; this is followed by the sharp and hard 't' sounds, which once again resemble the sound of someone striking metal; finally, the explosive and harsh 'd' sound at the end reinforces the idea that someone or something has been hit. The sounds in the word 'battered' therefore reflect the noises of multiple hits against an object, which would leave it exactly as the word describes: battered.

Test yourself (Technique)

Try to explain the effectiveness of the following sound effects.
1 the stuttering rifles' rapid rattle (Wilfred Owen)
2 sizzling sausages
3 The old road wound slowly through the hills.
4 Softly sleep stole over her.
5 little titbits

A whole technique PEEL might read as follows:

Q: How does the writer convey the fact that David is making a tremendous effort to lift the weight?

The author uses short sentences   `POINT`

like 'I raised my arms. I pumped them higher' to show David's   `EVIDENCE`
effort.

Short sentences here reflect how David tries in short bursts   `EXPLANATION`
to lift the heavy weight. The fact that he can only raise his
arms in short bursts shows how difficult the task is for
him. The full stops, where a reader would automatically take
a breath, match David catching his breath before the next
effort. As the breaths come often, much like panting, he is
obviously exerting himself.

So, by using short sentences the author shows that David   `LINK`
is making a huge effort.

Another PEEL, this time focusing on sound effects, might read as
follows:

Q: How does the poet make the coming of winter vivid?

Hughes makes the coming of winter effective by using   `POINT`
onomatopoeia,

saying 'the whistling green / Shrubbery are doomed.'   `EVIDENCE`

The 'w' sound of 'whistling' imitates the breath of wind   `EXPLANATION`
blowing through the shrubs and the cold hiss of the 's' sound
reflects the sound the wind makes as it rips through the
branches.

The use of onomatopoeia in 'whistling' is effective as it   `LINK`
shows the wind to be strong and cold at the onset of winter
as it blows between the branches of the greenery.

In Detail

The effect of common techniques

Many techniques – no matter where or how they are used – achieve the same effect each time. Thus, similes, metaphors and personification (also known as imagery) always seek to create a vivid picture in the reader's mind to make her or him better understand what the author is trying to describe.

But what about other techniques?

Here is a short overview of what some techniques usually do. In all cases, however, you will still have to explain why the author uses this effect and what it brings to the extract you are analysing.

- **Alliteration**: This can be used directly for the sound effect (as in 'the china chinked in the cupboard'), mirroring what is being described, much like onomatopoeia. Alliteration can also be used humorously, especially when overdone (e.g. The tiny troll threw a tantrum when it twisted its toes). Finally, through the repetition of sounds, alliteration is memorable and can be used for emphasis (e.g. crude and crunchy).

- **Capital letters**: These are used mainly either to emphasise words or because someone is shouting. The author obviously deems the words important (and you have to explain why that might be).

- **Commands (and exhortations)**: These are usually used in persuasive writing to get the reader to do something. They are a direct way of speaking to the reader and putting them on the spot, so that they feel the need to follow the command.

- **Exaggeration (hyperbole)**: This is usually used as a persuasive technique or to achieve a humorous effect, although it can be used for simple emphasis, too. As a persuasive technique, exaggeration can be used to describe the consequences of not adopting the writer's position (e.g. If you don't take action now, millions will starve). As a humorous technique, hyperbole is used to pretend things are worse than they are, which often makes them sound funny.

- **First person pronoun**: Using the first person plural pronoun 'we' is a subtle but very effective persuasive technique. When Henry V (according to Shakespeare) says on the field of Agincourt 'We few, we happy few, we band of brothers' he is suggesting that he is on the same level as every soldier and that every soldier is the same as him. The use of 'we' creates a team feeling, that we are all in this together.

- **Lists**: These show that there is a lot (often too much) of what is being listed and therefore adds to a sense of helplessness. Strangely enough, good things tend not to come in lists.

- **Repetition**: This works much the same way as alliteration in that it either emphasises certain words or phrases or makes them easier to remember. Repeating the same words again and again, at intervals, can also create atmosphere.

- **Rhetorical question**: This involves the reader by making them ask themselves a question. It can also be persuasive if the answer is obvious and the reader therefore is providing the answer in their head. This puts the reader on the same side as the author.

- **Rhyme**: Unless the rhyme is part of the formal necessities of a poem (e.g. a sonnet, which has a definite rhyme scheme), rhyme often contributes to the flow of a poem, making the sentences slip along more easily. Much like repetition, rhyme can also create a powerful atmosphere.

- **Short paragraphs**: These emphasise what is being said in the paragraph – the words are given their own space. Short paragraphs also tend to slow things down. A number of short paragraphs in immediate succession could suggest actions happening simultaneously.

- **Short sentences**: Especially when embedded in longer sentences, these stop the action and build tension. They slow down the pace of the story and highlight what is happening in that one sentence. They are a weaker form of the short paragraph.

- **Tense switch (usually to the present tense)**: If a story that is being told in the past tense suddenly switches to the present tense, this makes the action more immediate, as though it's happening now. It draws the reader in and makes them feel part of the action. It also makes memories more vivid.

Test yourself (Technique)

In the following examples name the technique and explain its effect. Use the list on page 19 for help, but remember to explain the effect of the technique in this particular example. Some examples may contain more than one technique; if so, you need only explain one.

1 If you do not donate money now, thousands of suffering children will starve.

2 The chicken whizzed around the farmyard like a formula one car with Grandpa hobbling behind, barely able to put one foot in front of the other.

3 I stumbled over the heath, all the time conscious that I was being watched. I turned around, but could see nothing through the mist. I stumbled on. Suddenly his eyes are in front of me.

4 You want to pass Common Entrance, don't you?

5 The gentle and green hills rolled to the horizon, like the lazy coils of a half-asleep dragon. Fences, hedges and rivulets criss-crossed the landscape, splitting it up and holding it together like sutures. Clouds scudded overhead, filtering the light of the sun to dusty fingers of grubby light that played across the fields. In the middle stood the house.

6 If we all work together, we can make it!

7 He twiddled his tagliatelle in the trattoria.

8 Come here, NOW!

9 The car was packed with suitcases, towels, shoes, various presents wrapped up in newspaper, pillows, boxes, a large picnic hamper, three dogs and the five of us.

10 So let freedom ring from the prodigious hilltops of New Hampshire. Let freedom ring from the mighty mountains of New York. Let freedom ring from the heightening Alleghenies of Pennsylvania! (Martin Luther King)

In Detail

Humour

Questions quite regularly ask about humour. Humour always stems from the contrast between what we expect and what happens. And even when we expect something to happen, it is often funny because we didn't expect it to happen in that way. The main techniques that are used to create humour are:

- **Irony** (or sarcasm) – using the contrast between what is being said and what is meant
- Various forms of **exaggeration**:
  - **Hyperbole** – building a contrast between what we think the situation would be and how it is retold
  - **Lists**
- **Pleonasm** – using more than one word which means the same thing, especially when one of the words is more unusual and therefore unexpected (e.g. He whooshed, galloped, dashed, darted and velociraptored home.)

Thought questions

Most thought questions ask about the character of people in the text. Usually the characteristics will not be spelt out in the extract – you have to infer them from the way the character behaves. In your PEELs you should use these clues as you quote and then explain – using common sense and your knowledge of the world and people – why this behaviour makes you think the character is as you describe him or her.

For example:

Q. What does the extract tell you about the girl?

The girl is obviously shy,   POINT

because 'when I asked her a question she flushed red before   EVIDENCE
turning away.'

When asked a question the normal, and polite, reaction   EXPLANATION
would be to provide some form of answer. The girl, however,
does not, but instead turns bright red. This suggests
embarrassment at being forced to talk and a lack of
confidence in what she has to say.

So, the fact that she turns red when asked a question   LINK
suggests she is shy.

Thought questions need not only be about character. They can ask you to express your ideas about anything to do with the text. When answering thought questions it is important that you refer closely to the text and base your arguments on it. When explaining, use common sense and state the obvious to lead the reader from your quotation to the point (as in the example above). Your explanation should be like the links of a chain holding the two together.

Try to explain which characteristic each of these sentences demonstrates.

1   His face flushed with bright crimson blotches, the headmaster turned to the boy and stared at him, wide-eyed, that he would dare to not eat up his food.
2   When the lunch bell rang, the children all sprinted to the dining room. Although Sophie was the first at the door, she held it open for the other pupils and went in last.

3   Macbeth knew he had been fooled by the witches and that he would probably die, but he attacked Macduff with ferocity nonetheless.
4   When his name was called, he stood up straight and marched up to the podium with huge strides, his eyes raised and his mouth fixed in a slight smile.
5   Although most of the villagers shunned him after the murder allegations were made, Helen still went to visit the old man.

Response questions

Usually the last question in a comprehension, a response question is a chance for you to bring in a bit of your personality and to write more freely about topics linked to the passage.

Response questions are asking for your engagement with the text in some way – either to comment on it or an issue raised in it, to continue it or to imagine you are part of the experience being described.

There is no set or structured way to answer this type of question. You should write what you think, but in as engaging and technically polished a way as possible. *Do* refer to the text in your answer, or use quotations, as this shows that you can use the text as the basis for your discussion.

If you are being asked to give your opinion, argue a case, or comment on a statement, you do not usually have to highlight both sides of the issue. For the purposes of the response question, a one-sided, possibly biased, piece will do. However, dealing with possible counter-arguments should gain you higher marks.

Writing accurately

Remember, in the exam you are trying to impress the marker. No matter how well you argue, you will fail to impress if you do not write accurately.

If you fail to write as accurately as possible you are giving your examiner the impression that you do not care about what you write – not something you want to do.

If you are unsure about grammar, use a textbook or ask your teacher to explain any rules you have forgotten or are not certain about.

In comprehensions it is advisable to write as accurately as possible from the outset, as you will probably have no time to review your work. Get into the habit of always writing as correctly as possible. This may take some time at first, but you will speed up as precision becomes second nature.

Timings

You have approximately 35 minutes to answer all the questions in each comprehension exercise. You will need about 4 to 5 minutes to read the text, bringing your total answering time down to 30 to 31 minutes. Given that the whole comprehension is worth 25 marks, you could say you have one minute per mark, plus a further 5 to 6 minutes (30 − 25 = 5; 31 − 25 = 6). As there are usually five or six questions overall, your time budget for each question is 1 minute per mark, plus 1 minute per question.

This means (as a rough guide only) that you should be able to answer a thought or technique question worth 6 marks in 7 minutes.

You can extend the time you have for the comprehension by giving yourself less time for the writing section. The suggested time for this is 40 minutes, but if you shorten that to 35 minutes, you have 5 minutes more for the comprehension. Ultimately, you will have to decide through practice which timings work best for you and stick to these in the exam.

Level 1 and level 2

Both comprehensions are available in two difficulty levels: level 2 is the standard, level 1 is simplified. At level 1:

- The text of the prose comprehension (paper 1) is usually shorter and contains more explanations of difficult words
- The questions are broken down more
- The questions offer more guidance
- You will usually receive more marks for points you make.

Comparison of level 1 and level 2

Level 2	Level 1
How does the author make the passage tense? (6) 3 PEELs; techniques must be named	Look at lines 10–23. Write down three things that build tension. (3) Specific section given; only quotations (evidence) needed
How does the poet create a vivid image of the mother? (6) 3 PEELs; techniques must be named	Look at the second paragraph. (a) Write down two quotations that create a vivid image of the mother. (2) (b) Explain what the quotations you have selected tell you about the mother. (4) Specific section given; 2 PEELs; PEELs broken down and worth 3 marks each
How do you think the narrator feels after the incident? (4) 2 PEELs; feelings must be named	After the incident the narrator feels angry (lines 11–16). Find two quotations that show this and explain your choices. (2+2) Specific section given; only 2 evidence (quotations) and explanations needed; guidance on feeling
How does the poet use imagery to bring the battle to life? (6) 3 PEELs; techniques must be named	Write down one example of personification (when an object is given human qualities) and one of a simile (a comparison, using 'like' or 'as') taken from lines 13–20. Explain why the poet might have used each one. (2+4) Specific section given; more guidance given; 2 PEELs; PEEL broken down; each PEEL worth 3 marks

This guide is mainly written on the basis of level 2 comprehensions. However, as the level 1 questions generally follow the same pattern and require the same skills to answer them, if you follow the advice given in this book, you should do well no matter which level you take.

2 Paper 1 Section A: Literary prose comprehension

There are four types of writing from which the texts for the prose comprehension can be taken:

- general fiction (novels and short stories)
- travel writing
- biographical writing
- plays.

Each one of these types has a distinct style. Knowing what is peculiar to each kind of writing makes it easier to find and discuss techniques and will also help you to understand what the author wants to achieve.

Fiction (novels or short stories)

This is a very broad category. Fiction can be based around historical events – such as the Middle Ages or the Second World War – or it can be about dragons and wizards; spaceships and robots; ghosts, werewolves or vampires or everyday life. What all the stories have in common is that they are made up.

The main purpose of any story is to entertain the reader. To do this, authors try to make their plots interesting and seek to immerse the reader in their characters and worlds. They do this by describing the world and what is happening in it as vividly as possible. They also tell the reader what their characters are thinking and feeling so the reader sympathises with and cares about them.

> **Key terms**
>
> A book-length story is called a **novel** and a shorter work of fiction a **short story**.

Expect many detailed descriptions, carefully selected words, as well as similes, metaphors, alliteration and onomatopoeia in literary fiction. Sentence length and structure will also vary, depending on what is being said: whenever the action gets tense, for example, authors tend to use short sentences and more paragraphs, while descriptions of settings are normally in longer sentences.

The writing is usually in the third person or in the first person (when an invented narrator tells the story) and in the past tense.

Sample text

The following example of literary fiction is taken from the novel *Life of Pi* by Yann Martel. In it the narrator is being shown around a bakery by the Muslim baker, when the call to prayer is heard.

> The baker interrupted himself mid-sentence and said, "Excuse me." He ducked into the next room for a minute and returned with a rolled-up carpet, which he unfurled on the floor of his bakery, throwing up a small storm of flour. And right there before me, in the midst of his workplace, he prayed. It was incongruous, but it was I who felt out of place. Luckily, he prayed with his eyes closed.
>
> He stood straight. He muttered in Arabic. He brought his hands next to his ears, thumbs touching the lobes, looking as if he were straining to hear Allah replying. He bent forward. He stood straight again. He fell to his knees and brought his hands and forehead to the floor. He sat up. He fell forward again. He stood. He started the whole thing again.
>
> Why, Islam is nothing but an easy sort of exercise, I thought.

Features of fiction

In the extract on the previous page:

- the author has included the thoughts and feelings of his main character, making him more likeable
- close descriptions bring the scenes to life
- dialogue adds realism
- the sentence structure varies depending on the sense and the effect required.

Travel writing

In travel writing the author writes about a place he or she has visited or a journey he or she has undertaken. The purpose of the writing is to make the readers experience the journey and the (foreign) places from the comfort of their armchair. In addition, the writer will seek to recreate some of his or her thoughts and experiences in the different places, and thoughts on what makes each place unique and different.

Travel writing can be either book-length or a shorter article in a magazine.

In Detail

When you read travel writing, expect a host of techniques designed to bring a place to life. This may be through techniques that focus on the sound of the words (alliteration, onomatopoeia, assonance), or through similes and metaphors and sensory language. Expect lists of all the things that are going on.

In addition to long, descriptive paragraphs, there will be musings on the character of places and people. These are the writer's own thoughts about what it felt like to be in the places being described and are the reader's window into both the foreign places and the author's mind.

Sometimes, especially at the beginning of a piece of travel writing, there might be facts and figures about the trip to root the piece in real life and to give a reference point to the reader.

Travel writing is usually in the past tense and in the first person, with the writer very much involved in the plot.

Sample text

The following extract is taken from the beginning of *The Bafut Beagles* by Gerald Durrell.

> Most West African lorries are not in what one would call the first flush of youth, and I had learnt by bitter experience not to expect anything very much of them. But the lorry that arrived to take me up the mountains was worse than anything I had seen before: it tottered on the borders of senile decay. It stood there on buckled wheels, wheezing and gasping with exhaustion from having to climb up the gentle slope to the camp, and I consigned* myself and my loads to it with some trepidation… Amid the rich smell of burning rubber, our noble lorry jerked its way towards the mountains at a steady twenty miles per hour; sometimes, when a downward slope favoured it, it threw caution to the winds and careered along in a madcap fashion at twenty-five.

(abridged)

*consign – to send (usually by post)

Features of travel writing

In the extract above:

- the author mentions the land and specific locational quirks
- the author uses anecdotes and understatement to make his experience humorous
- a number of literary techniques bring the start of the journey to life
- long sentences describe the lorry.

Autobiography and biography

Both biography and autobiography are book-length writings about someone's life. Both are therefore non-fiction (not invented).

Rather than just giving a list of dates and occurrences, good (auto) biography is a collection of memories or happenings that shaped the person's life.

The purpose of the writing is to entertain and to bring back, vividly, the various striking moments in the person's life, so that the reader can better understand the person and how he or she came to be such a person.

Key terms

In an **autobiography** the author tells about his or her own life; in a **biography**, someone else has written about the (usually famous) person.

In Detail

Biographical writing will usually be a mix of memories, often in the form of anecdotes, and commentary. In this sense it is similar to travel writing and many of the techniques employed will be the same (sensory language, similes, metaphors, emotional language). Expect more references to time and how things used to be in biography as well as – in autobiography – a more personal narrative voice. In addition, biographical writing may contain more irony, humour and dialogue.

Autobiographies are written in the first person, biographies in the third person and both in the past tense.

Sample text

This is an example of autobiography, taken from Roald Dahl's *Boy*.

> The sweet-shop in Llanduff in the year 1923 was the very centre of our lives. To us, it was what a bar is to a drunk, or a church is to a Bishop. Without it, there would have been little to live for. But it had one terrible drawback, this sweet-shop. The woman who owned it was a horror. We hated her and we had good reason for doing so.
>
> Her name was Mrs Pratchett. She was a small skinny old hag with a moustache on her upper lip and a mouth as sour as a green gooseberry. She never smiled. She never welcomed us when we went in, and the only times she spoke were when she said things like, 'I'm watchin' you so keep yer thievin' fingers off them chocolates!' Or 'I don't want you in 'ere just to look around! Either you *forks* out or you *gets* out!'

Features of biographical writing

In the extract above:
- the author mentions the year and the place in which this episode in his life happens
- a person is named and described vividly
- the point of view is very personal, with many emotions mentioned
- speech and dialect are used to show how the person talked
- only major or memorable moments are mentioned.

▶ Plays

Playscripts are very different from all the other categories of prose mentioned so far. One could argue that they are dead on the page, as they are written to be acted, to be seen. Nevertheless, you can also read a play – it just won't be as enjoyable as watching it.

When looking at a playscript you will immediately notice a number of differences: the playscript consists almost entirely of dialogue and stage directions.

The speech is assigned to the characters, whose names appear in the margin by the part they are to say. Shakespeare has very few stage directions; modern plays tend to have more. While plays can be written in verse or prose, modern plays are usually written in prose (and Shakespeare wrote mainly in verse).

Key term

Stage directions tell the actors and the director what is happening on stage. They are usually in italics and brackets.

In Detail 🔍

As playscripts are (mainly) dialogue, expect people to talk as they would in real life (especially in modern drama). This means there will be fewer literary techniques. What the characters say is the main way the audience can get a feeling of what kind of person each character is. Characterisation through dialogue – rather than similes and metaphors – is therefore an important element in this kind of writing.

Sample text

What follows is taken from Act 1, Scene 1 of *AD – The Early Years*, a play about the early life of Jesus by Edwin Morgan. In the extract, Jesus, aged 17, is talking to his father Joseph and his brother James.

JAMES   I'd like to teach. I could be good with young people.

JOSEPH   Teaching's not a man's job. Poring over scrolls, Mutter mutter mutter. Class rise, class sit.

JESUS   But what is a man's job? Is what a man does well not his job?

JOSEPH   Jesus, you ask too many questions. I know you want to defend your brother, but a father has to think of his sons' future. Builders will never be unemployed. A father has to guide.

JESUS   Everyone respects a father, and a father has to guide. But does a father have to command?

JOSEPH   Jesus, I listen to you, because you are not a namby-pamby like your brother. We have worked together on building sites in Nazareth, in Caesarea, all over, and I know you have a good eye and a strong hand.

JESUS   Even so, I may not be a builder for ever.

Features of playscripts

In the extract above:

- the language is simple and straightforward
- the characters do not necessarily speak in sentences
- colloquial turns of phrase are used
- the names of the characters are next to what they say.

Test yourself

Answer the following questions based on the short extract above.

Level 1

1 What job does Jesus have? What does James want to be?   (2)
2 Describe the character of Joseph.   (4)

Level 2

1 How do you know that Joseph thinks nothing of James's dream?   (6)
2 How does Jesus speak that reminds you of what he will be later?   (4)

3

Paper 2 Section A: Poetry comprehension

Most people find the poetry comprehension harder than the prose comprehension. This may be because you have not read much poetry. And when you read it, it probably seems complicated. This is because language is used in a much more daring way in poetry: pictures come thick and fast and the rules of grammar are often stretched to the limits. Words are left out and sentences are incomplete. Another difficulty may be the extreme focus on detail. A poem can spend half a page describing something as simple and seemingly uninteresting as a tree trunk. This level of detail, which we are not used to, can also make appreciating poetry difficult, especially when the poem suddenly moves from a detailed description to some philosophical musing. When reading poetry you need to keep an open mind that is ready for surprises.

However, don't be scared of poetry. It's all English and it all makes sense. Poetry does ask you, as a reader, to put more effort into your reading, to use your imagination to fill in gaps left by the poem. A poem does not usually tell a story in sequence, as prose does, but circles its objects with language. It is usually more thought and image than plot.

There are a few tricks to help you get to grips with poetry. Ultimately, the best way to grasp how poetry works is to read as much of it as possible. Familiarise yourself with the tips below and use them when reading poems.

Understanding poems

Reading to punctuation

The most important thing you need to bear in mind when reading poetry is that you should follow the grammar and not the line breaks. What you probably know of poetry is based on nursery rhymes or pop songs. These usually have a distinct rhyme and each line contains a thought. However, in most modern poetry, phrases do not end at the end of a line. So, unless there is a punctuation mark at the end of the line, don't stop there.

Take the following example:

> I remember one death in my boyhood
> That next to my father's, and darker, endures;
> Not Queen Victoria's, but Davidson, yours,
> And something in me has always stood
> Since then looking down the sandslope
> On your small black shape by the edge of the sea,
> – A bullet-hole through a great scene's beauty,
> God through the wrong end of a telescope.
>
> ('Of John Davidson' by Hugh MacDiarmid)

If you stop at the end of each line, parts of the poem won't make sense:

> I remember one death in my boyhood. That next to my father's, and darker, endures ... And something in me has always stood. Since then looking down the sandslope. On your small black shape by the edge of the sea.

Only by following the punctuation does the meaning become clear:

> I remember one death in my boyhood that next to my father's, and darker, endures ... And something in me has always stood since then looking down the sandslope on your small black shape by the edge of the sea.

An exercise you can do to help get this into your system is to find a partner and to read a poem aloud, changing reader at every punctuation mark (with the exception of apostrophes). This will help to bring out the sense of the poem as well as train you to read to the punctuation marks rather than the line endings.

Words can have more than one meaning

English words can be tricky to pin down: either because they have more than one meaning or because they can be used in more than one way. A verb can be used as a noun, a noun as an adjective, an adjective as an adverb – and so on.

Look at the following lines taken from the poem above:

> I remember one death in my boyhood
> That next to my father's, and darker, endures;

Key terms

Words that are spelt the same, but mean different things, like the various kinds of bow and pole, are called **homonyms**. Words that sound the same, but mean different things, like bored and board, are **homophones**.

'Endures' can mean either to suffer (e.g. the pain I had to endure) or to remain in existence (e.g. of all creatures only the rats endure). As it is the death that endures and it nowhere says what death might have suffered, it is clear that the second meaning is the correct one here.

Examiner's tip

As you can only recognise double meanings of words you know, make it a habit to use a dictionary to broaden your vocabulary.

Word order

It is interesting to note that while pupils have no difficulty understanding Yoda (of *Star Wars* fame), when he utters his Yodaisms, as soon as a poet does the same, no one understands. Word order in poems can be surprising, so while reading open keep your mind and work out what's what in a sentence.

In the poem on page 34 some words are not in the order you would speak them, as indicated by the arrows:

> I remember one death in my boyhood
>
> That next to my father's, and darker, endures; [...]
> And something in me has always stood
> Since then looking down the sandslope
> On your small black shape by the edge of the sea,

Missing words

Often poets leave out words that are grammatically necessary, but are not absolutely essential to understand the meaning.

For example, in the poem above the author writes:

> I remember one death in my boyhood
> That next to my father's, and darker, endures;

There is a word missing in this, as it should read: that endures next to my father's and is darker.

Key term

The technical term for leaving out words is **ellipsis**. This is also the name given to three dots …

Test yourself

Use the techniques above to transform these lines from Charles Causley's poem 'Manjimup' into more easily understandable lines.

At One Tree Bridge a single kookaburra

Machine-guns the noon light. The cormorant
Casts over the rigid pool its barb of eyes.
Somewhere beyond the rocks and rushes, a bright
Secrecy of maidenhair fern, the stream fidgets

Through sharp stones.

Reading for meaning

The best way to go about discovering what a poem is about (while also straightening it out in your head, as described above) is to read the poem a number of times. While reading, it is important to keep an open mind as to what the poem might be about; don't be quick to jump to conclusions and be ready to change your mind if something doesn't fit. Remember also to read the title; it is there for a reason.

Here is a suggested mode of attacking a poem:

1 Read the title of the poem and the poem once.
2 Think what the poem might be about. Use clues from the title and the text. Also use your knowledge of everyday life.
3 Using your first guess, read the poem again, checking whether the words of the poem support your idea. Be ready to discard an idea that does not fit the words. Do not force the words to say things they don't; don't think, 'It's poetry, words can mean different things there.' They can't and they won't.
4 Based on your second reading re-visit your ideas.
5 Read the poem sentence by sentence and find out what is going on in each. Remember: it's all English and all makes sense and will probably be about actions you can relate to either from your own experience or from reading or watching TV. When you string this together, you should have a good understanding of the poem.
6 Read the whole poem one last time and see how all the things you have discovered fit into place.

In Detail

See how the meaning unfolds in the following poem by Imtiaz Dharker:

First reading

This suggests the poem → is about something good.

There are four parts.

The poem is set in a dry area where there is never enough water.

There is something about people with buckets. Questions are: why do the people have buckets? Are they queuing for the little water there is?

Here children are screaming. Why is that? It seems this is because it is so hot that the sun is melting everything ('liquid sun').

Focus on these questions as you read the poem again.

Second reading

This marks a change, so something happens to the dryness.

As this is a poem about dryness, you can assume a water pipe has burst, meaning the water is lost.

The water is not seeping into the ground but spurting up, like a fountain. That's why the people are coming with pots and pans. They are collecting the water.

What's happening with the children? Even though they are in a separate stanza, the story continues with the sentence: the pipe is still burst and the water is spouting.

This is problematic. But you can also scream in joy – like at the funfair. Now everything fits: the children are bathing in the water, which is shining in the sun ('liquid sun') and the water covers them like a blessing.

Blessing

The skin cracks like a pod.
There never is enough water.

Imagine the drip of it,
the small splash, echo
in a tin mug,
the voice of a kindly god.

Sometimes, the sudden rush
of fortune. The municipal pipe bursts,
silver crashes to the ground
and the flow has found
a roar of tongues. From the huts,
a congregation: every man woman
child for streets around
butts in, with pots,
brass, copper, aluminium,
plastic buckets,
frantic hands,

and naked children
screaming in the liquid sun,
their highlights polished to perfection,
flashing light,
as the blessing sings
over their small bones.

So the poem is about a dry area, where there is never enough water. But when a water pipe bursts, suddenly there is so much water, it is like a blessing, and all the people come to collect it while the children play in the water fountain.

Literal and metaphorical meaning

A poem usually has (at least) two levels of meaning. Many poems appear to be about simple, everyday matters that are of no great interest. However, these are used to make a point about some basic truth of life. In a way it is like a conjuring trick: you think you are seeing one thing, which then turns out to be something very different. For example, you might read Blake's poem 'The Sick Rose' as being about a rose being attacked by a worm, but then realise that the poem is really about the dangers of obsessive love.

When first reading a poem, you should try to understand the literal meaning – what is actually going on. When you feel comfortable with the events being described, try to work out what (else) the poem is about.

As with all comprehension questions and answers, bear in mind that here, too, there is not necessarily a right or wrong answer. This sort of deeper analysis can form the basis for answers to response questions.

Test yourself

What do you think the following poem by Robert Frost is about, both literally and metaphorically?

The Road Not Taken

Two roads diverged in a yellow wood,
And sorry I could not travel both
And be one traveller, long I stood
And looked down one as far as I could
To where it bent in the undergrowth;

Then took the other, as just as fair,
And having perhaps the better claim,
Because it was grassy and wanted wear;
Though as for that the passing there
Had worn them really about the same,

And both that morning equally lay
In leaves no step had trodden black.
Oh, I kept the first for another day!
Yet knowing how way leads on to way,
I doubted if I should ever come back.

I shall be telling this with a sigh
Somewhere ages and ages hence:
Two roads diverged in a wood, and I—
I took the one less travelled by,
And that has made all the difference.

Techniques in poetry

Poems often have a whole host of techniques packed into just a few lines. The main techniques you will encounter in poetry are the same as in other texts: metaphor, simile, alliteration, assonance and onomatopoeia. However, these techniques will be used more densely in poetry.

In addition, poetry makes use of rhythm and sometimes rhyme (although a lot of modern poetry tends not to rhyme).

Rhythm

One of the main factors that distinguishes poetry from prose is its rhythm. Classically, poems had a distinct and usually very regular rhythm. In modern poetry this traditional use of set rhythm patterns (known as metre) has been softened and poets now try to capture the natural rhythm of speech.

Rhythm is an inherently tricky thing to analyse. However, there are poems that have a strong rhythmical element to them, which underlines and strengthens what the poem is saying. You should be able to pick up on the rhythm and explain how it contributes to the effect of the poem.

So, how does it work? The rhythm of a poem is based around stressed syllables. Words with more than one syllable have a natural stress and therefore it is easier to see the stress in these words.

For example, in:
- 'butterfly' the first syllable is stressed: BU–tter–fly
- 'locomotion' the third syllable is stressed (with a possible stress on the first syllable, too): lo–co–MO–tion
- 'tonight' the second syllable is stressed: to–NIGHT.

Knowing this, the line:

> The butterfly will sing tonight of multicoloured dreams residing in a crawling shell

has the following stresses (rhythm):

> The BU-tter-FLY will SING to-NIGHT of MUL-ti-COL-oured DREAMS re-SI-ding IN a CRAW-ling SHELL

Discovering a line's rhythm is not easy. In the following examples the rhythm is more obvious and contributes directly to the effect of what the poet is trying to convey.

Consider these lines by Lord Byron:

> The Assyrian came down like a wolf on the fold,
> And his cohorts were gleaming in purple and gold;
> And the sheen of their spears was like stars on the sea,
> When the blue wave rolls nightly on deep Galilee.

Each line here has the same, distinct rhythm. It goes like this:

> The As-SYR-ian came DOWN like a WOLF on the FOLD

Explaining the effect of this rhythm could read like this:

> Byron is describing the attack of the Assyrian army and uses the strong rhythm of his lines, which sounds like horses galloping (ta-ta-DUM repeated four times per line) to underline the speed and strength of the attack: the rhythm makes the attack sound inexorable and unavoidable, as though nothing can stop the army.

The following lines are from W.H. Auden's poem 'The Night Mail':

> Letters of thanks, letters from banks,
> Letters of joy from the girl and the boy

The rhythm here is

> LE-tters of THANKS, LE-tters from BANKS
> LE-tters of JOY, from the GIRL and the BOY

The effect can be explained as follows:

It is not absolutely regular, but the rhythm quite clearly matches the di-di-DUM sound a train makes as its wheels roll over the rails and the spaces between them. The rhythm underlines what the poem is about, giving the reader a real feel for the night mail speeding along the tracks.

Test yourself

Try to find the rhythm in the following lines:
1   Sparrows fly in circles round the window
2   If I knew what I wanted my life would be much easier
3   Carnivorous dinosaurs avoided prehistoric vegetation
4   The way the whale swims through the sea will always be a mystery
5   Never say you will come on time if you have difficulties to appear

In Detail

Generally speaking, rhythm usually has one of the following effects:

- **emphasis**: by stressing certain words, the poet can make them stand out more. It is also possible to draw attention to words by making them break an otherwise regular rhythm.

- **atmosphere**: rhythm can add to the atmosphere, as in the examples above. Without such a strong rhythm, what the poet is saying would not be as memorable or effective.

- **flow**: a steady or regular rhythm can help a poem flow, which might be important for what the poet is saying. However, too regular and racy a rhythm can also distract from the words: think about the lyrics that pop songs get away with – just because they have a racy rhythm!

Metre

If a poem has a regular rhythm throughout, we speak of metre. Metre is built up of elements of rhythm that are repeated a certain number of times in a line.

There are four types of feet in English poems:
- **iambs** (ti-TUM) – tonight, as a word, is an example of an iamb
- **trochees** (TUM-ti) – e.g. window
- **dactyls** (TUM-ti-ti) – e.g. butterfly
- **anapaests** (ti-ti-TUM) – e.g. understand.

In Detail

Poetry can be described in terms of the types of feet and the number of feet (and beats) in a line:

- He WORE his SCAR-let CLOAK
  is an example of iambic **trimeter** (three feet).
- The As-SYR-ian came DOWN like a WOLF on the FOLD
  is an example of anapaestic **tetrameter** (four feet).
- MA-ny SOL-diers DIED to-DAY in BA-ttle
  is an example of trochaic pentameter (five feet).

Note that the feet do not have to match word boundaries: a word can be split into two feet, as 'scarlet', 'Assyrian' and 'today' all are in the examples above.

Rhyme

Rhyme is not quite as difficult to spot as rhythm, as it usually sits at the end of the line. However, it can be quite well hidden, either because the rhyming lines are far apart, the lines only half-rhyme or because the rhyme is hidden within the line (internal rhyme).

Two lines of poetry that rhyme with each other are called a rhyming couplet. They are quite common.

The lines of Lord Byron quoted on page 40 are in rhyming couplets.

Half rhyme

Words that don't quite rhyme are half rhymes, such as 'tune/moons' or 'hurt/lurk'. A special case of half rhyme is the consonant rhyme, where the consonants are the same, but not the vowel, like 'pots/pets'.

Test yourself

What kind of rhyme (pattern) do the following words or lines have?

1 bough/cow

2 Colonel Fazackerley Butterworth-Toast
  Bought an old castle complete with a ghost
  (Charles Causley)

3 The Hart loves the high wood,
    the Hare loves the hill,
  The Knight loves his bright sword
    the Churl loves his bill
  (Anon)

4 short/chart

5 I went down to the river's edge
  To see what I could see
  But all I saw was grass and trees
  And endless miles of hedge

In Detail

The effect of rhyme, much like that of rhythm, can be any one (or all) of the following:

- **emphasis**: by making certain words rhyme, the poet can make them stand out. We tend to remember rhymes, so making words rhyme – especially in an unusual way – makes them memorable.
- **atmosphere**: when words that have a particular sound are rhymed with each other, they strengthen this sound and create an atmosphere.
- **flow**: lines that rhyme speed the poem along. As soon as you know that lines rhyme you tend to hurry the lines to the rhyme, making the poem flow.
- **structure**: more complex rhyme schemes can also bind the lines more tightly together, bringing a structure to the poem it would not have without the rhymes.

Form in poetry

A number of types of poems have a set shape, a strict way a poet must write them. We call this form. Form usually revolves round stanza patterns. There are many different forms of poems. Two are still quite common today: the sonnet and the ballad. However, most modern poems no longer follow these classic forms.

> **Key term**
>
> In poetry, verses (or 'paragraphs') are called **stanzas** or staves.

Stanzas

Stanzas can either be regular or irregular. When stanzas are regular it means that they are all constructed in the same way: they might all have five lines of which lines one, three and five rhyme as well as lines two and four; the rhythm will also be the same. Irregular stanzas are all different: there is no set principle according to which they are all built.

The ballad stanza

The ballad stanza is not a poetic form as such, but a certain way of writing a stanza. It was and is used a lot for songs and stories. The ballad stanza consists of four lines; the first and third line have four stresses and the second and fourth line rhyme and have only three stresses. This makes for a good narrative rhythm, as the following example (by Charles Causley) shows:

> She said the Caistor sky was blue,
> The wind was never cold,
> The pavements were all made of pearl,
> The young were never old.

The sonnet

The sonnet is a poem of fourteen lines with a set rhythm and rhyme pattern. While the rhyme pattern can change, the rhythm is usually iambic pentameter (five stresses per line). In more modern versions of the sonnet form, the rhymes are not always full rhymes, but can be half rhymes or consonant rhymes. So the main thing to look out for is fourteen lines.

A sonnet is usually written about one idea, such as love or loss. Shakespeare wrote 154 sonnets. A more modern sonneteer is Edna St Vincent Millay (who wrote 178), but many modern poets have written sonnets.

The following is Millay's most famous sonnet. Note the fourteen lines, the rhyme scheme and the rhythm as well as the topic.

> What lips my lips have kissed, and where, and why,
> I have forgotten, and what arms have lain
> Under my head till morning; but the rain
> Is full of ghosts tonight, that tap and sigh
> Upon the glass and listen for reply,
> And in my heart there stirs a quiet pain
> For unremembered lads that not again
> Will turn to me at midnight with a cry.
> Thus in winter stands the lonely tree,
> Nor knows what birds have vanished one by one,
> Yet knows its boughs more silent than before:
> I cannot say what loves have come and gone,
> I only know that summer sang in me
> A little while, that in me sings no more.

Sample text 1

Using all the techniques acquired in this chapter, read through the following poem and see if you can discover what it is about. When you feel you have a good understanding of the poem, attempt the sample questions.

I like to see it lap the miles
And lick the valleys up,
And stop to feed itself at tanks
And then prodigious step

Around a pile of mountains,
And supercilious peer
In shanties by the sides of roads,
And then a quarry pare

To fit its sides
And crawl between
Complaining all the while
In horrid, hooting stanza,
Then chase itself down hill

And neigh like Boanerges*,
Then prompter than a star,
Stop, docile and omnipotent,
At its own stable door.

by Emily Dickinson

* Boanerges means sons of thunder

Sample question and answer

Do you think the ending is effective? Explain your reasons in detail with reference to the text. (4)

Note: This is a thought question with 4 marks, meaning the answer should contain two PEELs.

Yes. I think the ending is very effective. The final two lines of the poem starts with the word 'stop' which – set in commas as it is – brings the flow of the poem to an abrupt halt. This is effective as the train has reached its destination and so stops. The poet makes the poem mirror this, which is a vivid way of making the reader realise the train has halted and of closing the poem.

The poet hints that the train has reached home 'its own stable door'. This is a good ending as it suggests that the inanimate train has now gone to rest as any animal would. The poem ends on a note of tranquillity after the bustle of the previous stanzas, much like a real train journey, making this a fitting end to the poem.

Test yourself

Answer the following questions based on the poem on page 45.

Level 1

1 In the poem Dickinson compares a steam train to a horse. Find and write down two examples of this.   (2)
   Explain why you think the poet might have done this.   (2)
2 In your own words describe the journey the train makes.   (4)

Level 2

1 How does Dickinson make her description of the steam train effective?   (6)
2 In what way does the form of the poem help us imagine a train?   (4)

Sample text 2

Now read through the following poem.

Roman Wall Blues
Over the heather the wet wind blows,
I've lice in my tunic and a cold in my nose.

The rain comes pattering out of the sky,
I'm a Wall soldier, I don't know why.

The mist creeps over the hard grey stone,
My girl's in Tungria*; I sleep alone.

Aulus goes hanging around her place,
I don't like his manners, I don't like his face.

Piso's a Christian, he worships a fish;
There'd be no kissing if he had his wish.

She gave me a ring but I diced it away;
I want my girl and I want my pay.

When I'm a veteran with only one eye
I shall do nothing but look at the sky.

by W. H. Auden

* Tungria is a part of modern Belgium

Test yourself

Answer the following questions based on the poem on page 47.

Level 1

1 The poem is written in rhyming couplets (every two lines rhyme). Why do you think the poet may have chosen to write his poem like this? (4)

2 Imagine you are a Roman a soldier on Hadrian's Wall. What would you complain about? Try to key into the mood of the poem in your answer. (5)

Level 2

1 The Roman soldier is obviously not happy about his situation. Write down three quotations that tell you this. (3)

2 What impression do you have of the narrator? Refer to the text to explain your ideas. (6)

4 Section B: Writing tasks

Although the tasks set in the writing sections of Papers 1 and 2 are very different, both are about writing well. The basics of this are universal.

The writing sections

Each Section B contains a number of writing tasks, usually set in the form of titles. Each section carries 25 marks.

In each section you are required to write one essay or story only.

The paper assesses your use of language: both the basics of English (grammar, spelling and punctuation) as well as the original and engaging use of a style that fits what you are writing.

You have 1 hour 15 minutes to complete each paper, so around 35 to 40 minutes to plan and write each Section B response.

Paper 1: Section B

This section asks you to write prose for a practical purpose. This can be to advise, argue, explain, inform or persuade. There are usually three different titles from which to choose.

Two further titles ask you to argue a general point about reading, using books you have read to support your view.

Paper 2: Section B

This section contains a choice of four titles, one of which is usually split up into three sub-titles, on the basis of which you are meant to write creatively, either a narrative or a description, imaginary or real.

Language basics

In the writing sections in particular you are trying to impress your marker with how well you can use English. No matter how well you write stylistically, poor spelling, grammar and punctuation will ruin the impression you are trying to make.

Punctuation

Make sure that every sentence starts with a capital letter and ends in a full stop. This is an absolute minimum requirement.

Grammar

Make sure your sentences all make sense. Unless you are doing it on purpose, for effect, you should always write in full sentences. You need to take particular care when constructing more ambitious sentences.

Avoid the following common mistakes:

> *Being in different places that seem so much bigger than what I was used to towered over me.*

Here the sentence has changed direction in the middle: after 'what I was used to' the sentence should have continued with something like 'scared me', but the second half concludes a sentence that was never started about the buildings in the bigger places.

Don't change idea mid-sentence. Finish each idea in its own sentence.

> *To this day I still remember how cocky I was and how the old saying pride comes before a fall.*

This sentence is obviously incomplete: words are missing at the end, something like 'is true'. Make sure you finish your thoughts and your sentences.

> *Still not quite understanding when the man took the keys and started the car.*

This is once again a fragment and an example of a particularly common mistake. The sentence starts with a participle group (around 'understanding'), but this needs to refer to a subject in a main sentence, which doesn't exist. Adding 'I watched him drive off without stopping him' would make the sentence complete.

> *There are electric aeroplanes, puppets and more but the one thing that caught my eye, a teddy bear.*

Examiner's tip

If you have difficulties remembering full stops, try getting into the habit of putting a dot on the paper before you raise your pen to think what to write next.

Key term

A **fragment** is an unfinished piece of writing. Grammatically this usually means an unfinished sentence.

Here there is a verb missing in the main clause: adding a 'was' and deleting the comma before 'a teddy bear' solves this problem.

All alone on the very bottom shelf, all alone.

This is once again a fragment: something is missing at the end; 'the puppet stared into the glassy distance' added onto the end would turn this into a sentence.

Walking past shops, the pavement was cracked and broken.

The participle construction (around 'walking') refers to the pavement, which is quite obviously not walking. 'Walking past shops, I noticed the pavement was cracked and broken' would be correct.

Test yourself

Turn the following into complete sentences:
1. I never knew where I was so as soon as I could get in touch with the people in my country all I wanted is them to take me home.
2. Gun bullets going everywhere, people screaming and the robbers shouting at the clerks behind the bank desks.
3. The person in the bag is pinned to the floor and threatened to be killed unless a couple of thousand pounds is brought to him.
4. People try to escape through the back and bang three people moving like a stone.
5. The park as dark as death surrounded.
6. Snowflakes attracted magnetically to the icy floor.

Spelling

Make sure you do not misspell any words that are on the paper. They are directly visible in front of you and ignoring them is careless.

While this guide cannot and does not intend to give an overview of spellings, bear in mind these common misspellings:
- An **effect affects** someone.
- **They're** is short for they are and **their** means belonging to them; if neither of these is intended, then use **there**. (**You're** and **your** are similar to they're and their.)
- **It's** is short for it is or it has. **Its** means belonging to it (e.g. its claws).
- **Two** is a number, **too** means as well or shows excess or muchness (e.g. too much); if you mean neither of these, use **to**.
- Should of (or would of or similar) does not exist; it is **should have** or (less formally) **should've**.

Test yourself

1 Fill in the correct word – they're, their or there:

_____ are three boys and _____ playing with _____ ball and as _____ kicking it around _____ is a policeman standing _____ and watching _____ antics.

2 Fill in the correct word – to, too or two:

_____ have _____ people more in this lifeboat would mean there are _____ many people in the boat for it _____ reach its destination, which is still _____ days away.

3 Fill in the correct word – its or it's:

_____ late and the beast polishes _____ claws as _____ going hunting to feed _____ family.

How to write well

Writing well primarily means using the specific techniques associated with each genre – and using them well. However, there are a few common elements that apply to all kinds of writing. Practise these beforehand so you know how to use them in the exam.

> **Key term**
>
> **Genre** is a category of story or writing that follows certain rules and conventions, which make it recognisable (e.g. ghost story, review).

What to avoid

Try not to use 'There was/were/is/are'. These are dead words. Rephrasing sentences with these words in them makes the sentences much more exciting.

> There was a yellowing skull staring at me from hollow eyes

could become

> A yellowing skull stared at me from hollow eyes

> There was a large meadow behind the house

is better as

> Behind the house a large meadow stretched to the horizon.

Don't use familiar or colloquial phrases, other than in dialogue.

Don't use more words than you have to. Aim to keep your writing tight and not to repeat or waffle.

> **Key term**
>
> **Colloquial language** is everyday, informal language. This is the way most people talk. It is often used in dialogue to add realism or to show character.

Look at the following example:

My fingers felt like ice and were black. They dug themselves into the ground. It was like they were trying to strangle the life out of the snow – that is if the snow would have had any life.

This can be tightened as follows:

My black, icy fingers dug into the ground, trying to strangle the snow.

Test yourself

Tighten the following passage:

My legs lay twisted beneath me. Something had happened to them; some dreadful thing, which was sharp and painful, seemed buried underneath their skin. This thing must have happened while I was falling down the face of the mountain. That must have been some time around 2 pm, just before the storm struck. And all I could think of was the pain and whether it would go away. I tried to think of other things, but it was useless: the fire in my legs was too strong.

What to do

Make sure that you use a variety of verbs that say exactly what you want. If you use the right verb, you often need very little else to bring a sentence to life. If possible avoid simple verbs such as 'got', 'were' (and all other forms of 'to be') and 'have'.

Sentence length

Vary the length of your sentences. Nothing is duller than always using the same type and length of sentence. As a rule of thumb, use longer sentences to describe setting and scenery and use short sentences for rapid action or for effect. It is also a good idea to progressively shorten sentences that are about the same thing: so, start off with a longer sentence and then shorten the length for the next sentence and so on. This can of course also be done in reverse. The main thing is that your sentences change length.

For example, don't write:

> On the hill I saw the church. It was squat and grey like a toad. Behind it clouds scudded across the dark sky. I approached. Singing emanated from the building. Lights glowed in the windows. I walked towards the door.

Instead, join the sentences together to make more effective sentences of different lengths.

> On the hill I saw the church, squat and grey like a toad, highlighted against the clouds scudding across the dark sky. As I approached I heard singing emanating from the building as light glowed in the windows. I walked towards the door.

Note how the sentences become shorter as the description progresses. The reverse – making the sentences become longer – could read like this:

> On the hill I saw the church. It squatted grey like a toad in front of a dark sky with scudding clouds. As I approached, singing emanated from the building and lights glowed in the windows, making me hasten towards the door.

Paragraphs

Make sure you use paragraphs. Current practice is to use too many rather than too few paragraphs. Whenever you start a completely new topic in your writing, you should use a paragraph. Paragraphs are also used to mark a shift in time or speaker. Paragraphs can also be used for emphasis, to highlight certain words or phrases. A one-sentence or one-word paragraph can be highly effective.

Honestly.

More sophisticated punctuation

Try to use more sophisticated punctuation. Full stops, commas and apostrophes should all be correctly used. Think about using brackets (parenthesis) and ellipses (…) as well as colons (:), semicolons (;) and dashes (–).

- **Colon**: this punctuation mark says, 'What is after me is an example of what is before me.'
- **Semicolon**: this joins two complete sentences into one. The two sentences must be closely related and not joined by a conjunction. You never have to use a semicolon: a full stop or a conjunction can do the trick. Stylistically, a semicolon is often better.
- **Dash**: this is used for emphasis. It can replace brackets, commas or a colon. In direct speech dashes can also be used to show pauses or interruptions.

Although you should use literary techniques appropriate to the task, there is one technique that merits a mention here, as it is so universal and important: the tricolon. The tricolon is a three-unit pattern or a group of three. It is used by many writers, is not hard to master and will improve your own writing style. That was a tricolon. As is this:

He was battered and beaten and knocked about.

Paper 1 Section B: Writing for a purpose

This section asks you to write for a purpose, either to argue, persuade, explain, advise or inform, or you can write about books.

Each one of these types of writing has a distinct style and makes use of certain techniques. You need to know these in order to write a successful piece in each genre. For all these types of writing you should write in a formal style, avoiding colloquial language.

Planning

Before you begin, you should plan. Remember the plan is for you. It is not for the marker (your plan does not get sent to the senior school) and not for your teacher. Only write down what will help you.

The plan will help you structure your essay, find a conclusion and keep track of where your essay is heading, making it clearer and allowing you to develop ideas. See pages 98–104 for a number of different planning templates together with examples.

In Detail 🔍

How to plan

1   Write the title of your essay at the top of the planning sheet; this will help focus your thoughts.
2   Brainstorm points you can raise, if appropriate, both for and against the issue, or scenes you can use (for the book essay).
3   Order your scenes or arguments (on each side) according to strength. There are many ways to do this. One way is to start with the second strongest and continue with weaker and weaker arguments, but end with the strongest argument; another way is to start with the weakest argument and to get stronger and stronger.
4   To plan your conclusion find out what all the scenes or arguments (on one side) have in common; do this for the other side too, if applicable. Compare the common ground found or compare in what way the scenes or arguments deviate from the common ground. The main factor that differentiates the scenes or points or that influences why each argument is different is the basis for your conclusion. For more detail on writing conclusions, see the section on pages 71–72.
5   Start writing. You do not need to plan the introduction as you know what the essay is about, what you will write and where it is leading you.

Beginnings

No matter what type of essay you are writing, you can begin them all in much the same way.

Q. Imagine you are writing an article for the school magazine on the dangers of extreme sport.

Here are a number of ways to begin:

1 Your own experience related to the topic in question

Think of something that happened to you that relates to the title and write this down as your introduction. Make sure you provide enough detail to make the account vivid and credible.

> *Although abseiling may not be the most dangerous sport, in my experience it is dangerous enough. The first time I went, I was nervous, but managed to slide down the inside of the water tower without mishap. When I had hard ground beneath me I wanted to get out of the harness as quickly as possible. So I touched the hook to release the ropes – and burnt my hands. Most of the time the dangers of extreme sport are greater, though.*

2 A current affairs or historical link

If you can think of a story that has been in the news lately or of some historical happening that links in with the title, then you can start with that.

> *At the Historic Dockyards in Medway they are offering bungee jumping for charity: you get people to sponsor you for recklessly jumping into thin air with only an elastic band as a safety line and all you have to do is take the plunge. While it is debatable whether bungee jumping is a type of sport, extreme experiences are becoming more of an everyday event.*

3 A definition of the main points of the title or question

This is particularly useful if the title contains words that aren't clear. By defining them you are stating clearly what you will be discussing, making it also easier to follow your arguments.

> Extreme sports are those which involve a large risk and only insufficient safeguards against these. So, while mountain climbing itself is not an extreme sport, mountain climbing with no equipment, just bare hands (so-called free climbing), quite definitely is. Typically, only a small group of people carry out extreme sports and these people need the adrenaline rush of putting themselves in peril.

4 A proverb or saying

If you can think of a saying or proverb that somehow fits the title, this can be an original way of starting.

> 'Look before you leap' is the moral of one of Aesop's fables, in which a fox entices a goat to jump into a well so it can get out as the goat is jumping in by running along its back. Now, while extreme sport enthusiasts are not necessarily trying to persuade us to join them in their perilous pursuits, they do carry out their sport on the back of society, as we have to step in to rescue them if something goes wrong.

5   A cultural link

Much like the current affairs or historical link, you can also use a reference to a cultural icon, such as a painting or a building.

> One of the most enduring and tragic myths is that of Icarus, who, when fleeing Crete with his inventor father on wings made of bird feathers and wax, flew too close to the sun. This caused the wax to melt and the boy to plummet to his doom. In a way this tragic story has similarities with extreme sports today, where people often undertake daring stunts in homemade contraptions, with sometimes similar results.

6   A repetition of the title in your own words

This is the least exciting of beginnings, but at least it is a beginning and it will focus your mind on the question.

> The risks of hobbies or other free time activities that put the person doing them in grave peril are a topic worth considering. Does the fun these people get out of the extreme sports justify the risks they take?

The ways to start listed above work no matter what type of prose for a purpose you choose.

Examiner's tip

Remember to dive straight into your introduction. If you look at all the examples in this section, they get to the point immediately. Do the same.

Test yourself

Try writing all six kinds of introduction (and the introduction only) for the following title:

School uniform should be abolished.

Writing to persuade

Here you are trying to convince the reader of your opinion or to do something. Advertising is a very simplified (but effective) form of persuasive writing. When you are writing persuasively, your writing will be biased. However, you also need to deal with counter-arguments and show why they are of no relevance.

Text sample

Q. Write a letter to a newspaper persuading it that Latin is an important subject.

Part of the main response to this title might read:

> Surely everyone can see the benefits of learning Latin. Without Latin we run the risk of forgetting who we are. Latin helps us unlock documents of the past and engravings on tombstones, church walls and public monuments. We are who we are through our (shared) memories. Do you really want to be cut off from the past and become a nobody?
>
> There are some who maintain pupils should learn a modern language instead, as Latin is dead. How misguided! Latin opens the door to more languages than any other. But Latin is so much more than just a language: it also trains logical thinking. Instead of puzzling over a Sudoku, translate some Latin and reap multiple benefits.

Examiner's tip

Imagine you are actually writing for a specific person whom you are trying to persuade. This will help you think of and focus your arguments.

Structure

After writing the introduction go through your points, according to strength. If you do not end with your strongest point(s), then you can repeat your two strongest points at the end.

Deal with counter-arguments as you make your points and sandwich them in between your own points of view.

Examiner's tip

Never leave a counter-argument unanswered.

In Detail

Techniques

Persuasive texts are biased and emotional and seek to convince and draw the reader in.

Use the following techniques:

- Address the reader directly, using either 'you' or 'we'.
- Appeal to the reader's emotions.
- Use rhetorical questions.
- Use words like 'surely', 'everyone knows' and 'obviously' that suggest everyone agrees (when they don't necessarily).
- Use commands.
- Use repetition to emphasise and drive home a point.
- Make use of a PEEL structure to detail your arguments.
- Use short punchy sentences to make a point.

Sample questions

The following question types are ones which require a persuasive response:

- Write a letter to the headteacher persuading her or him to cancel lessons on snow days so pupils can enjoy the snow.
- Write an article for a newspaper persuading readers to adopt a healthier lifestyle.
- Write a note to your parents persuading them to give you more pocket money.

Writing to argue

This type of writing is about presenting arguments for and against a certain issue. Bear in mind that depending on how a question is formulated, your position (pro or con) may shift. In your essay you should discuss both sides and then draw a conclusion stating which side has the better arguments; you can also add your personal opinion.

> **Key terms**
>
> The arguments for a certain issue are also known as the **pros** and those against as the **cons**.

Text sample

Q. School drama productions don't actually teach pupils any drama: they are self-serving vehicles for the rare few pupils who can act. Discuss.

Part of the main response to this title might read:

> School productions are not just for the stars. While it is true that they are an opportunity for pupils more interested in dramatics, they are a great opportunity for the whole school to work together at a great outcome. From the seemingly most insignificant singer in the choir, who stands in the last row on stage and can barely be seen, to the stage hands who never show their face to the audience, each pupil is a necessary part of a great happening. Without every pupil the production would be a different one. So far from it being just for the stars it is a true community effort that involves all and teaches all pupils – from stars to stage hands. Drama is an enterprise in which all are dependent on others and success comes only from cooperation.
>
> As harmonious and noble as that sounds, school productions are less about explorative and cooperative dramatics and are often dictatorial events, where one overloaded and overworked member of staff barks out orders to all children in a time-pressed frenzy of trying to set up a half-way decent production in which parents can admire their little darlings. And to that extent it is only about the pupils on stage and the more on stage you are, the more it is about you. It is those that have the most lines, that are on stage the most, the leads, that the parents will talk about, that will be remembered for their part in the production, not the lighting technician or the set painter. Therefore, school productions only serve to put the few that seek the limelight into it.

Structure

After the introduction develop all the arguments for one side, starting a new paragraph for each main point. Then detail the arguments for the other side.

Don't mix up the arguments for each side.

Examiner's tip

In your conclusion, as well as mentioning your own opinion, try to find some middle ground between the two sides, some new way that takes both sides into account.

In Detail

Techniques

Discursive texts are impartial. As such, they should not take sides.

Use the following techniques:

- PEEL for each argument you make. State the main thrust of your point, give an example and then explain how that example is relevant or highlights the point you are making.
- Don't bring yourself into the essay. Use the passive voice to keep an impartial style.
- Do use persuasive techniques to make your points more convincing, but be careful not to overdo them: you want each argument to sound persuasive and valid, but you don't want to sway your reader in one direction or the other.

Sample questions

The following question types are ones which require a discursive response:

- Single sex schools are better for learning than mixed schools. Discuss.
- Creative lessons like drama, art and music, are more important than academic lessons. What do you think?
- Pupils should have an active say in how their school is run. Write an article for your school newspaper, highlighting both sides of the argument.

> **Key term**
>
> A **discursive** essay is the formal written discussion of a topic.

Writing to explain

Here you are trying to make something clear to the reader. Writing to explain often involves an expert telling amateurs how something works. It is all about providing necessary detail in a way that is easily understandable.

Text sample

Q. Do you have a pet? Explain in detail how to look after it.

Part of the main response to this title might read:

> Cats are not so much pets as house owners who tolerate servants, which is what you are. The first step to looking after a cat is understanding that the cat is not there for your pleasure, but you are there for the cat's. If you internalise this, it will make life with your cat much easier.
>
> The most important duties you have are feeding, cleaning and grooming.

Cats do not eat huge amounts in one go, but like to nibble bits every now and then. A full food bowl at all times is therefore important. I find that having dry food out at all times and feeding wet food at certain times to complement this suits my cat best.

Structure

After the introduction make sure your explanation follows a logical structure. Start with general statements and become more detailed as you go along. The conclusion should summarise the main points briefly.

In Detail

Techniques

Explanation texts should be impartial and should provide clear details. If there are various different ways of doing something, the text should give clear information on the pros and cons of each possibility. Although the text should be mainly impersonal, it is possible to bring in personal experience and opinion.

Use the following techniques:

- Use a clear structure. This may involve using headings and sub-headings, bullet points or fact boxes, where appropriate.
- Make sure your writing is clear and that you are not using complicated language.
- Don't use over-long sentences.
- Highlight and explain key words.
- Include personal experience, if relevant.
- Base your explanations on facts.

Sample questions

The following question types need an explanatory text as response:

- Do you have a favourite gadget? Explain to someone who has never heard of it what it is, what it does and how to use it.
- Explain your hobby.
- What is your favourite sport? Explain its rules. Imagine you are writing for someone who does not know the sport and has never played it before.

Writing to advise

In this kind of writing you are using your knowledge to help someone else make a decision. You not only have to list the choices on offer and the pros and cons of each choice, but also try to match each alternative to the preferences of the person being advised.

Text sample

Q. Advise a friend what to wear to his grandfather's birthday party.

Part of the main response to this title might read:

> You have a basic choice of casual or formal wear.
>
> As it's your grandfather's birthday party, I would think that a more formal approach would be appropriate. So that means definitely no jeans. Trousers can either be grey or dark blue flannels, corduroy, moleskin or similar. You should definitely wear a shirt. This should not have any strong colours in it.
>
> Depending on how formal the occasion is, you might have to wear a suit or jacket and tie. If you're invited to someone else's house I would suggest a slightly smarter look than if you are just going out to eat. However, if it's a whole party that's organised at a hotel, for example, then dress as elegantly as possible.
>
> The best thing to do is check with your father what he will be wearing and then copy that as best you can.

Structure

After the introduction make sure your advice follows a logical structure. Go through the different possibilities, making sure you leave nothing out. The conclusion should give your personal idea of what it would be best to do and why.

In Detail

Techniques

Advisory texts should be impartial and provide clear details. If there are different ways of doing something, the text should give clear information on the pros and cons of each possibility. Although they should be mainly impersonal, it is possible to bring in personal experience and opinion.

Use the following techniques:

- Use a clear structure. This may involve using headings and sub-headings, bullet points or fact boxes, where appropriate.
- Make sure your writing is clear and that you are not using complicated language.
- Use PEELs to develop your points.
- Don't use over-long sentences.
- Highlight and explain key words.
- Include personal experience, if relevant.
- Base your explanations on facts.

Sample questions

The following question types should be answered with advisory writing:

- Imagine you have been asked to help a new pupil choose two extra activities. What would your advice be?
- Someone wants to spend £5000 and is asking for your advice. What should she spend it on?
- Advise a fellow pupil on what pet they should purchase.

Writing to inform

Here you are giving more facts or details about a certain occurrence or subject. Once again, it is key that you are clear about what you are writing and deal with all possibilities. Some forms of autobiographical writing could be placed in this category.

Text sample

Q. Write a short report about a place you have visited.

Part of the main response to this title might read:

> Most tour operators in Morocco offer a trip to the Sahara. They advertise for this trip with a photo of a huge sand dune that burns a bright orange in the sunlight. So, like so many others, I booked the trip to the desert.
>
> I expected waves and mountains of sand stretching hot and inhospitable to the horizon. However, the day was spent travelling through a lunar landscape: dusty land littered with

little rocks. What most people don't know is that the desert you find in Morocco is a stone desert: stretches of dull, flat, dusty ground strewn with stones and rocks. Every now and then a tree will rise out of the parched ground and in that tree invariably a goat will be feeding. Rocks and rocks and some thorny trees. Not a dune in sight.

Well, there is one dune: the one from the photo. In the midst of the stone desert there is in fact one sand dune – huge and out of place. You have to take great care when taking a picture of it that you crop your image so it looks like you've actually been in the sand desert, when all you ever saw was one big dune.

Structure

After the introduction make sure your information follows a clear, logical structure. Describe and write about all the important detail. In the conclusion sum up the most important facts of the main part and point the reader in the direction of further sources of information.

Techniques

Writing to inform should be matter-of-fact. Although a more personal style is possible, remember that your main purpose is to provide information and knowledge.

Use the following techniques:
- Use a clear structure with headings and sub-headings, if appropriate.
- Use literary techniques to put your message across, but do not let them get in the way of the facts.
- Keep your style matter-of-fact and as impartial as possible.
- Include tips or personal experience, if relevant.

Sample questions

The following question types require writing to inform:

- Write a pamphlet for new pupils to your school informing them about the most important things they need to know.
- Write about a time when you made the wrong choice. How did it come about and how did you know the choice was wrong?
- Imagine you are your form representative. Tell your form what the last meeting of the school council decided upon and why.

Writing about books

This is not a category of its own, as such, as it can include writing to advise, argue, inform or persuade. The main difference is that here you should use books as evidence for the arguments you are putting forward.

Text sample

Q. Do you prefer books in which a lot happens or more slow moving ones? Explain your views using one or more books you have read.

Part of the main response to this title might read:

> In quest or adventure books there is seldom a moment in which nothing happens. Moments of calm reflection are few and the hero battles more than thinks. In Michelle Paver's 'Wolf Brother', a novel set in a Stone Age imbued with magical elements, Torak, the hero who is on a quest to destroy a demon bear, is constantly facing some new danger. Even in the lifeless Arctic he almost falls down a ravine, has to dodge a sudden mini-avalanche and survive a snow storm. The only chance he has to think about what to do next is when he shares a meal with his companions. And while these scenes of shared thoughts and companionship outline character, they are merely short (and somewhat dull) respites before the next bout of action. It is the action, the scrapes, near misses and close escapes, that make 'Wolf Brother' such an enjoyable read. Were nothing to happen on the quest, only the slow forging together of an inseparable team through long discussions, the book would lose all excitement and be of small interest to me. So, at first glance I would say that I definitely prefer a book in which a lot happens.

Structure

Each paragraph should provide an answer to the question being asked or highlight the issue from a different angle. This should be done by discussing one scene in the book in a bit more detail (but don't re-tell the whole story) and using this to argue the point. In effect, you are PEEL-ing in each paragraph, using a scene from the book as your evidence. In the conclusion you should not only state your own opinion, but explain what the scenes you used have in common and where they differ, and why.

Examiner's tip

Start each paragraph with a topic sentence, which is a clear statement of the point you are making.

Which books to select

It is advisable to choose works of fiction, as these are easier to write about because they have their own stories. However, if you feel a factual book would suit your response better, feel free to use that.

Choose books you know well. The better you know your books, the easier you will find it to write about them. It is a good idea in your essay to refer in detail to two books. You can then perhaps refer to a third (or fourth) briefly.

When thinking about which books to use, try to select a classic and a more contemporary book. Shakespeare is always impressive, of course, but any classic novel, such as *Lord of the Flies*, is suitable.

Examiner's tip

Write the title of books in inverted commas and capitalise the initials of each (longer) word. For example:

'The Old Man and the Sea'

Presenting key scenes

In the course of your essay you will be using scenes from books you have read. Use the present tense when re-telling these. When presenting your scenes, make sure you introduce the book first: give a short summary of the setting and the main characters, so that the scene you describe is easy to follow. (You do not need to introduce Shakespeare's plays.)

An example of a book introduction is:

> 'Private Peaceful' is a novel about two brothers, Charlie and Tommo, who grow up in the country and then go off to fight in the First World War together.

Examiner's tip

Keep book introductions short. A long introduction will slow down the flow of your arguments.

Test yourself

Try writing short book introductions for some of the books you might use in a book-based essay.

Sample questions

You can expect the following question types for writing about books:

- Moments of crisis bring out a person's true character. Have you found that to be the case in books, too?
- Books make you forget the world around you. Write about a book that made you forget the world.
- Anyone who has not cried at least once when reading a book has never read a good book. Is this statement true of you?

Helpful words and phrases

Linking words	Contrasting words
firstly/my first point is	in contrast
most importantly	on the contrary
leading on	on the other hand
also	conversely
similarly	however
in a similar vein	be that as it may
following on from that	despite what has been said
of equal importance	although
likewise	in comparison
moreover	whilst
furthermore	unlike
in addition/additionally	

Words to lead into the analysis	Words for the conclusion
this suggests	as can be seen from the above …
this demonstrates/shows	to conclude, I think that
this keys in to the idea of	what all points have in common is
from this we can infer	as the arguments show/prove
looking carefully at the scene, we see	on balance, I believe
consequently	in conclusion
thus	in summary
therefore	finally
undoubtedly	

Conclusions

Generally, every conclusion should provide two things:

■ a summary
■ an outlook.

As a rule, the following applies:

Writing:	The conclusion should:
• to persuade • to explain • to inform • to advise	• sum up the main points • show a way forward
• to argue • about books	• point out the underlying issue • throw a different light on the issue

The summary stems from what you've written (or planned) and the outlook is your personal view. The conclusion for discursive essays and essays about books are more difficult to plan than essays in which you are writing to persuade, explain, inform or advise, as you have to try to find an underlying issue, if possible. This will depend on careful and extensive planning.

For example, imagine you are planning a discursive essay on 'The whole world should speak English' and you have the following arguments for each side:

Pro	Con
Internationally most spoken language	People won't give up national language – part of their identity
Easy to pick up	Spellings difficult to master
Grammar not hard	English almost global second language, doesn't need more
Already wide distribution through music	Forcing language on others will not be welcomed
Would lead to better understanding between people	Esperanto failed

With these arguments, the question is what is the underlying issue – what is it really about? There is no one single answer to this. Answers could include: establishing peace, maintaining stability, cultural identity. Each one of these issues underlines the whole debate and at least one (of your choice) should be mentioned in the first part of your conclusion.

The second part might then focus on what other initiatives might be more important to secure world peace.

The conclusion could read as follows:

> All discussions about one unifying language for the world are driven by the desire to achieve perfect communication between all the people on earth in the hope that this will tie them closer together and prevent hostilities. However, such endeavours do not take cultural differences and questions of identity sufficiently into account. Indeed, all attempts to create a single global language have so far failed. So it seems better to expend money and energy in finding other ways to further world peace and cooperation than games with languages.

Or consider the following title: 'Is it ever right to kill someone?' Your plan might be as follows:

Pro	Con
If you have been captured and would be tortured, but you can kill your jailer, then you would and should	Even if someone kills someone else, you should not kill them, because then you're on their level
It would have been right to kill people like Hitler or Stalin, who caused the deaths of millions	Even if a person asks to be killed (euthanasia), what if that person changes their mind at the last minute?
If you are at war, you have to kill the other side	Death penalty also not right – the state should not kill anyone, as this suggests it can be right to kill

Find out what all the scenes or arguments (on one side) have in common. And then do the same for the other side.

On the pro side, the killing of one person is to stop greater pain or death or to save one's own life. On the con side, the bottom line is that while someone else might take their own life away, no one else can do that or should be allowed to do that as life is sacred.

This is the basis for the conclusion: is life always sacred or can you say it is better to take one life than let thousands suffer?

Test yourself

Write the conclusion for the essay 'Is it ever right to kill someone?' that has been planned above.

Mark scheme

The exam board provides a mark scheme. It is useful to know what markers are looking for, as this will help you improve your writing.

Mark	Descriptors	
	All writing tasks	**Writing on books**
1–11	Not relevant to the chosen task; with little attention to detail;	Knowledge and understanding of the text(s) not relevant to the task;
	clarity weak owing to poor organisation and technical inaccuracy; very short and undeveloped.	
12–15	Generally relevant to the task; some attention to detail; style and tone generally appropriate for the chosen task;	Knowledge and understanding of the text(s) generally relevant to the task; some reference to the text made to support ideas;
	ideas clearly communicated and organised into paragraphs; spelling sufficiently accurate.	
16–19	Mainly relevant to the task; structured in an effective and interesting way; good attention to detail; style and tone adapted well for the chosen task; a good range of vocabulary and expression;	Knowledge and understanding of the text(s) mainly relevant to the task; good reference to the text to develop ideas;
	ideas clearly communicated; well-structured essay; spelling generally accurate.	
20–25	Consistently relevant to the task; ideas developed fully and well-structured in an original and stylish way; excellent attention to detail; essay much enhanced by style and tone; spelling consistently accurate; a wide range of vocabulary and expression.	Knowledge and understanding of the text(s) consistently relevant to the task; sound insight shown; close reference to the text to develop ideas fully; ideas clearly communicated; detailed and well-structured essay; spelling generally accurate; a good range of appropriate vocabulary.

Relevance to task

This area of the mark scheme relates to whether the essay is answering the question. Are the points dealing with the topic? Does the evidence being used relate to the title? It is important that you do not go off track, but keep your essay focused on the title at all times.

Structure

Your essay should have a clear introduction, main part and conclusion. These parts should not only be visible and recognisable, but should also fulfil their function well. Within the main part, your essay should also be structured so that individual points flow from one to the next and are easily picked out.

Use paragraphs to make the structure visible. If your writing needs a special layout (like a letter) then make sure you use this in the exam.

Your essay should be long enough to enable you to deal with the topic in sufficient detail and to make your line of argument clear.

Examiner's tip

If you are unsure about how long your essay should be, write four fully developed PEELs in the main part; if writing about a book, three PEELs, each one based on a different scene, is sufficient.

Technical accuracy

To gain high marks it is vital that your basics of grammar are correct. Capital letters and full stops are an absolute minimum, but apostrophes, commas and speech marks should also be used correctly.

Spelling

Your basic spelling should be accurate – you should not misspell common words. If you are unsure of a spelling, make sure it is phonetically correct so that the reader can see which word you meant.

Examiner's tip

If faced with the choice of using a more advanced word that you're not sure how to spell and a simpler word that you can spell, go for the more advanced word and spell it as best you can.

Clarity

Make sure your argument is clear and that you are writing it in a clear manner. Don't construct sentences that are so long that either you or the reader gets lost. Plan your conclusion so that each of your points builds up to it.

Vocabulary

Use words that fit what you are saying. If you are arguing a complex point that requires a lot of thought, it will not impress if you use very simple language. The more precise your choice of words, the better.

Examiner's tip

Articles in newspapers, especially those in the commentary section, use words that are useful for each genre. Read as many comments in good newspapers as you can and try to acquire the range of words used there.

Reference to text

This applies only when writing about a book.

You should use the scenes to develop your argument. Bear in mind, therefore, that the scenes are there to support what you have to say and are not the main focus of what you write. Make sure your choice of scene fits the title and your purpose. Do not simply re-tell the story; mention only as much of the scenes as you need to make your point.

Attention to detail/development of ideas

How well do you know what you are writing about? You should provide in-depth arguments that show you have a good understanding of the main issues at stake. This means that you should not necessarily go with the first points that come into your head, but use the planning time to think of what lies at the core of each topic.

For example, a discussion about school uniform is not mainly about looks or comfort, but about individuality and conformity.

Style and tone

Make sure you write in a formal style. Avoid colloquial language. The techniques you use and the way you write should fit the genre in which you are writing.

Test yourself

Write a response to any of the example essay titles given under each genre of writing and use the mark scheme on page 73 to see how well you did. You could do this with a revision partner so someone else marks your essay.

6

Paper 2 Section B: Creative writing

This section asks you to write creatively. Its purpose is to let you show how well you can write. You can write either a story or a description, the main difference between the two being how much plot is involved. In both types of writing you should use language to the best of your abilities.

Choosing a title

Roughly 80 per cent of all pupils choose the same or the same two titles. This means you will stand out if you choose a different title. However, it is better to write well on a title with which you are comfortable than to write badly on a title no one else has chosen.

When you see the titles, decide which ones you feel you can write about. If there is only one, take it. If there are a number, choose the one you think no one else will write about.

What to write about

How much should you write? Aim to write one and a half pages, two if your handwriting is large. Anything longer than three-quarters of a page should allow you to write an acceptable response.

When choosing a topic, you should write about something you have experienced. This does not mean you have to write autobiographical accounts, rather that you should use your experiences to write about similar situations. For example, in order to describe flying realistically, use your experience of cycling, putting your hand out of a car window and walking along cliff tops, as well as observations of birds.

When describing emotions, stick to those you have experienced, otherwise your writing will sound false. As you write, re-live your feelings so that you can describe them in detail.

> **Examiner's tip**
>
> THE BIGGEST SECRET: No one is interested in your story. No one wants to read it. You have to write in such a way that people will want to read it.

> **Examiner's tip**
>
> If possible, don't go with your first choices. Take time to think about alternatives.

> **Examiner's tip**
>
> As a general rule, if you write too much, it will be badly written.

How to make your writing original

Even if you choose a popular title, there are a number of ways of making your story original.

Change the point of view

The point of view, or pov, is the angle from which you see the story – the eyes and mind through which you experience it. Usually these are human eyes. But you can choose to tell your story from the point of view of any creature or object.

This is not easy as you have to decide how much you want to 'be' the animal or thing. A good approach is to think which senses would be used and to describe most of the world through these senses. Also, try to invent a few words that might suit your creature's or object's world view. To change the pov you must know a lot about the being you are inhabiting.

The following extract is written from the point of view of a fruit machine. Although the machine is given thoughts like those of a human, its character and horizon are those of a machine.

> The day started like any other: people fed me milled and smooth discs, the suns of my existence, then pulled my arm to make my stomach churn. Some pulled with a prayer, some pulled in concentration, some pulled with feigned nonchalance. But as soon as the rolls rumbled in my bowels, their expressions all became the same – fixed and frozen. As light after light flashed and the music of my stomach shifted and shunted and still no need, no urge to spill developed, I became cocky, realising all those coins would be mine, mine, mine. No-one was going to take them from me. For this one day, the money would all be mine.

Examiner's tip

'But now everyone who has read this book will do the same and I won't be original any more!' you might complain. That's possible (though you'd still be original). But most pupils, in the heat of the exam, forget this advice. Make sure you're not one of them.

In Detail

If you are using a different point of view, bear the following in mind:

- Which senses can you have and use? Focus on these and describe the world mainly through these.
- What can you know? If you are a rat, you will know nothing of cars, for example. To you they would just be noisy monsters that every now and then claim a rodent life.
- Make sure the story fits the world of your new point of view. So, if you are a virus, you are not likely to go shopping.

Re-interpret the title

Don't let yourself be bound by most people's understanding of a title. Most people will think the title 'The Disused Station' refers to a train station, but you could write about a space station, a research station or a police station.

Another way of re-interpreting a title is by assuming one of the words is the name of a creature. 'Spring is Here' could be used as the title for a story about your first pet rabbit, which you decided to call Spring.

You can interpret the title metaphorically. For example, 'The Tunnel' need not be about an actual tubular length of darkness, but could be about a stretch of time in which the character faced a whole string of difficulties.

Test yourself

Think of original ways to re-interpret the following titles:
1 My Family
2 Journey to London
3 Shopping
4 Trapped
5 The Cascade

Stream of consciousness

Instead of writing a straightforward story you could write an essay that follows someone's thoughts. This is called stream of consciousness writing. The difficulty is keeping to thoughts only. You cannot portray action directly – only indirectly through the thoughts that result from activity.

The following extract is a stream of consciousness of a pupil in the lunch queue.

Hmmm. That doesn't look too good. Bet the meat's stringy. What else is on offer? Jacket potatoes. Had one of those yesterday … Come one, get a move on, get a move on, get a move on. I have other things to do than stand here. Have to get to music practice … Why is the canteen always slow? They should have two people dishing out food, not just the one. Tray. Wet. Always wet. Why are trays always wet? 'Why with the power of the death star do we not have a tray that is dry?' Brilliant sketch, that. Oh, me!

In Detail

If you are writing a stream of consciousness, bear the following in mind:
- This type of writing uses a lot of fragments, questions and ellipses to mirror (interrupted) thought processes.
- While the writing can be somewhat informal, make sure it is not too colloquial.
- The writing typically jumps from one topic to the next, much as the mind does.

▶ Planning

Planning consists of two steps: brainstorming and sequencing events. The purpose of the first is to collect ideas, the purpose of the second to order these into a timeline. A story that will be written in 30 minutes does not need a lot of planning. Most of it can be done in the head. There are good reasons to plan the sequence on paper, though. Most importantly, your plan will tell you when to stop and what you are writing towards.

Key term

Brainstorming is writing down ideas that come into your head. The results are often charted in the form of a spider diagram or concept map. Remember this is not a sequence of events which you can immediately use to write your story.

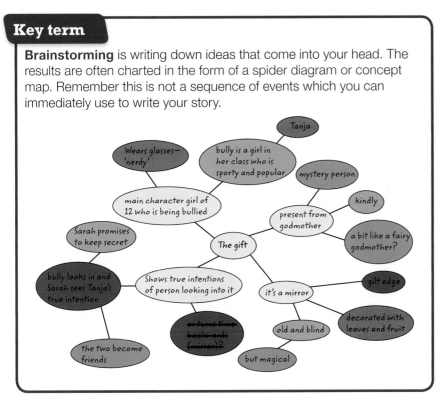

When sequencing, plan your ending first. Then go one step of action back from your ending and start your story there.

For example, imagine you are sequencing a story with the title 'Over the Hills':

End: I set off over the hills

I'm a bird that's hatched and is ready to migrate, but scared of journey, doesn't know what to expect – only heard rumours of what's over the hills, but doesn't know

Beginning: first birds leaving on migration, the pull inside me, they tell me to join

Starting with the narrator hatching would be too long and ambitious a story. This plan is manageable, especially if written well with descriptions, thoughts and feelings.

Writing

How to begin

It is important that your beginning grips the reader as quickly as possible. There are a number of tricks to help you do this.

Start with	Example and effect
Dialogue	**'Over here, Pete!' Carol cried excitedly.** Dialogue puts the reader into the middle of the action. What is being said also builds curiosity – the reader wants to know what Carol has found.
Onomatopoeia	**Creeeech! With a sharp scream the wheels gripped the tarmac as the car sped round the corner, trying to evade its pursuers.** The use of sound effects pulls the reader into the story and again into the middle of the action, making the reader wonder what is going on.
Setting	**The hotel stood alone at the end of a promontory which jutted out into the wild waves and howling winds of the Atlantic: a last beacon of humanity facing the riot of the elements.** This is a calmer way of beginning. However, if you describe your setting well, it should engage the reader.
A mystery	**No one was quite sure why the lights were always on at night in the deserted church.** Starting with something that is outside the usual course of events will make the reader wonder why this is and want to read on.

Examiner's tip

Use a question near the beginning of your story to hook the reader. The question will make the reader wonder, too.

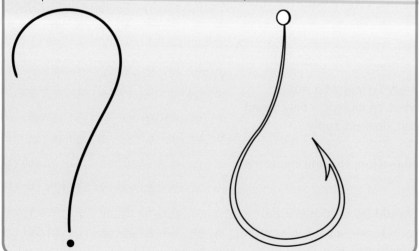

Test yourself

Use the plan on page 79 for the story 'Over the Hills' about the migrating bird and write four different beginnings for the story using the methods described in the table.

The action tap

When writing your story, you should include one event, with an appropriate build-up and release. Use the idea of the 'action tap', where your writing is like a drop of water forming and falling.

THE ACTION TAP

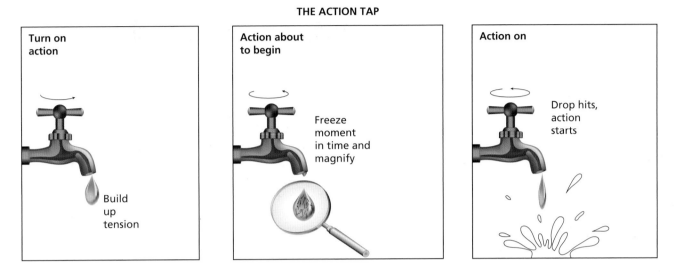

At the beginning, use a number of literary techniques to make the drop build up: emotions and feelings as well as a definite mood will help, as will little hints and uncertainties in the plot itself.

Then, when the drop is ready to go, when the tension has been sufficiently built up and is just about to be released, stop time for a moment and focus on the detail. Describe the second before the action starts in detail – the sound, the feeling, the 'eternal second'.

Then let time run its course as the drop hits the water and action resumes.

What to include

Depending on whether you are writing a description or a story, what you include will be slightly different.

In a descriptive piece you will have little action (although you do need to have some form of movement through your description), but a lot of description as well as thoughts and feelings as reactions to what is being described.

In a story you should include description, action, thoughts and feelings and some dialogue. While there is no ideal mix, description should be the main part of what you write, even when telling a story. This is because description allows you to show what you can make language do.

Descriptive techniques

No matter whether you write a description or a story you will need to use a range of descriptive techniques, such as onomatopoeia, alliteration, similes and metaphors. Good imagery is vital. You can tell a good simile or metaphor because it will work on various levels.

For example:

> The marine crept forward as flat as a plate.

This simile only tells us that the marine is flat, because that is the only similarity between marine and plate. The marine is neither brittle nor round, nor is he used to eat from.

> The marine crept forward like a snake.

This simile, though simple, has more depth and is therefore better. Not only does the comparison to the snake suggest movement close to the ground, it also carries elements of camouflage, stealth and deadliness, all attributes the marine also has.

Writing good similes and metaphors takes practice. The more you write them and think about them, the better you'll get.

What to avoid

Only include information and scenes that move your story forwards. Leave out everything that is not necessary. Don't include getting up, washing, brushing your teeth, having breakfast – unless they are vital for your story.

Avoid scenes involving blood. As you will have no experience (let's hope!) of shooting at someone, being shot or using any other form of weaponry, don't write about it. You won't be able to do so convincingly.

If you write your story in the first person, don't die at the end. How could you be writing the story?

Don't end with waking up and it all having been a dream.

Mark scheme

Pupils often ask, 'What do I get marks for?' or 'Will I lose marks if I don't use paragraphs?' You have to bear two things in mind: in your writing task you are being assessed on a number of different things at the same time and there is no central institution marking all CE papers – your senior school will mark your paper.

The ISEB has a suggested mark scheme. There are no set marks for doing certain thing, but rather bandwidths, in which you are expected to demonstrate certain skills. So, if you do not use paragraphs, it does not automatically mean you are in the 1–11 mark section. If you are doing all the other things mentioned in the 12–15 segment, you may get 13 or more marks, as only one element is missing. To a certain degree it will depend on how important your marker thinks paragraphs are.

Mark	Descriptors
1–11	Not relevant to the chosen task; clarity weak owing to poor organisation and technical inaccuracy; very short and undeveloped with little attention to detail.
12–15	Generally relevant to the task; ideas clearly communicated and organised into paragraphs; some attention to detail; style and tone generally appropriate for the chosen task; spelling sufficiently accurate.
16–19	Mainly relevant to the task; ideas clearly communicated and well structured in an effective and interesting way; good attention to detail; style and tone adapted well for the chosen task; spelling generally accurate; a good range of vocabulary and expression.
20–25	Consistently relevant to the task; ideas developed fully and well structured in an original and stylish way; excellent attention to detail; essay much enhanced by style and tone; spelling consistently accurate; a wide range of vocabulary and expression.

Relevance to task

Make sure, if you are re-interpreting the title, that it is clear you are still writing to task.

Clarity

Don't get caught up in your plot; stick to your plan to make your story as clear as possible.

Attention to detail

Use literary techniques to bring your story to life and focus on detail when describing the outside world as well as emotions. For example, use:

- powerful and unusual words – no slang
- precise verbs
- adjectives and adverbs
- sensory language
- images (similes and metaphors)
- alliteration, assonance and onomatopoeia.

But don't overdo it!

Instead of writing:

I was angry

write

Heat flushed to my face as my stomach knotted tightly and my hands involuntarily clenched into fists. I would get him, I swore to myself. I would get him.

Style and tone

Use a variety of sentence openers and connectives and vary your sentence length (use simple, compound and complex sentences).

See pages 73–75 for more detailed explanations of the terms used in the mark scheme.

7

In the exam

As the structure of both papers is identical (a comprehension exercise followed by a writing exercise), these guidelines are applicable to both papers.

First steps

1 Make sure you have enough space around you so that you can write easily and see the question paper at the same time. Get rid of any unnecessary equipment and clutter.
2 Apart from your pen, have a spare cartridge as well as a spare pen and a pencil (if all else fails) to hand.
3 Make sure you have enough paper – both for planning and writing.
4 Make sure you can see a watch or clock when you look up.
5 As a guideline, you have 35 minutes to complete Section A and 40 minutes to complete Section B. You can change these times according to what works best for you. Whatever your decision, make sure you note down the time when you need to switch to the second section.

Section A

Before you start writing

1 Read the passage or poem once, carefully, trying to understand as much of it as possible. Also try to get a feel for the structure of the passage: what is mentioned where.
2 Read through all the questions for the section carefully.
3 Quickly scan through the passage again and make notes of areas to which the questions refer.

This should not take longer than 5 minutes.

> **Examiner's tip**
>
> It is better to spend a bit longer on reading and making sure you understand the text than to rush the reading and misinterpret the passage.

Answering

1 As you come to a new question read it again carefully to make sure you understand it.

2 Look at the number of marks the question carries and decide on how you will answer the question based on the marks assigned and the question type – make brief notes (e.g. 'three PEELs') if necessary.

3 Answer in full sentences. Write your answer as fully but as briefly as you can. Do not repeat yourself. Only answer the question. Structure your answer by starting a new paragraph for each PEEL.

4 Make sure that for each PEEL you have at least the point and evidence written down so you get no fewer than half marks for each one.

5 If you are stuck on a question, leave a space to answer it and move on to the next. Do not waste time trying to answer a question you don't understand.

6 If you are nearing the end of the time allotted for the section and you haven't answered all the questions, jump to a question that you feel confident you can answer correctly.

7 Only if you are running out of time, answer in bullet points rather than full sentences.

Examiner's tip

Don't aim to get full marks, but try to get all the marks you can. Do little things that might get you an extra mark, or even a half mark.

At the end

1 Check through your work and make sure that what you've written answers each question and that you've tailored your answer to the marks available.

2 Check through your work and make sure you have written full sentences and that they start with capital letters and end with full stops.

3 Check your spelling, punctuation and grammar.

Often you will not have time for these three steps at the end, so make sure you write as accurately as possible right from the start.

Examiner's tip

The most important thing is that your answers make sense.

Section B

You should leave between 5 and 10 minutes for planning and about 5 minutes at the end to read through your answers again. This means you have roughly between 25 and 30 minutes to write your essay.

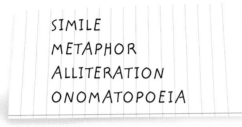

SIMILE
METAPHOR
ALLITERATION
ONOMATOPOEIA

1 As soon as you have a piece of paper, fold it to make a stand. Write simile, metaphor and any other relevant literary techniques on it. Every time you look up, include one of the techniques in your writing.
2 Read all of the questions before deciding which one to answer. Think carefully about the title you are going to write about. Choose one that 'resonates' with you.
3 Underline the key words you are being asked to write about.
4 Plan your answer in detail. Also brainstorm sophisticated and adventurous vocabulary you could use.
5 Remember to write the number of the question you are answering at the beginning of your response.

At the end

1 Read through your answer again and check that what you have written makes sense and answers the question.
2 When you read through what you have written you should feel proud of what you have produced. If you have the feeling that something is not quite right, change it!
3 Check your spelling, punctuation and grammar. If you find spelling difficult, make sure your attempts are phonetically correct.

> **Examiner's tip**
>
> If you read through the sentences from the end of your answer to the beginning you will pick up more mistakes.

8 Practice paper

This section contains a full mock Common Entrance paper, much as you will receive in the actual exam. The order is the same as in the exam and a layout has been selected that works optimally for level 2 candidates, with comprehension questions facing the text. Level 1 candidates can photocopy their questions, so that they, too, have text and questions facing each other.

General information on the exam:

- You have 1 hour 15 minutes for each paper. This includes time for reading the passages, taking notes and planning.
- In each paper, answer **all** the questions in **Section A**, but only **one** question from **Section B**.
- Technical accuracy (spelling, grammar and punctuation), word choice and presentation are all important and will be taken into account.

Paper 1, Section A: Literary prose

My First Peregrine

I saw my first peregrine on a December day at the estuary ten years ago. The sun reddened out of the white river mist, fields glittered with rime, boats were encrusted with it; only the gently lapping water moved freely and shone. I went along the high river-wall towards the sea. The stiff crackling white grass became limp and wet as the
5   sun rose through a clear sky into dazzling mist. Frost stayed all day in shaded places, the sun was warm, there was no wind.

I rested at the foot of the wall and watched dunlin feeding at the tide-line. Suddenly they flew upstream, and hundreds of finches fluttered overhead, whirling away with a 'hurr' of desperate wings. Too slowly it came to me that something was happening which
10   I ought not to miss. I scrambled up, and saw that the stunted hawthorns on the inland slope of the wall were full of fieldfares. Their sharp bills pointed to the north-east, and they clacked and spluttered in alarm. I followed their point, and saw a falcon flying towards me. It veered to the right, and passed inland. It was like a kestrel, but bigger and yellower, with a more bullet-shaped head, longer wings, and greater zest and buoyancy
15   of flight. It did not glide till it saw starlings feeding in stubble, then it swept down and was hidden among them as they rose. A minute later it rushed overhead and was gone in a breath into the sunlit mist. It was flying much higher than before, flinging and darting forwards, with its sharp wings angled back and flicking like a snipe's.

This was my first peregrine. I have seen many since then, but none has excelled it for
20   speed and fire of spirit. For ten years I spent all my winters searching for that restless brilliance, for the sudden passion and violence that peregrines flush from the sky. For ten years I have been looking upward for that cloud-biting anchor shape, that crossbow flinging through the air. The eye becomes insatiable for hawks. It clicks towards them with ecstatic fury, just as the hawk's eye swings and dilates to the luring food-shapes of
25   gulls and pigeons.

To be recognised and accepted by a peregrine you must wear the same clothes, travel by the same way, perform actions in the same order. Like all birds, it fears the unpredictable. Enter and leave the fields at the same time each day, soothe the hawk from its wildness by a ritual of behaviour as invariable as its own. Hood the glare of the eyes, hide the
30   white tremor of the hands, shade the stark reflecting face, assume the stillness of a tree. A peregrine fears nothing he can see clearly and far off. Approach him across open ground with a steady unfaltering movement. Let your shape grow in size but do not alter its outline. Never hide yourself unless concealment is complete. Be alone.

J.A. Baker

Level 2

Read the passage entitled 'My First Peregrine', which is taken from *The Peregrine* by J. A. Baker, and then answer the following questions using complete sentences. The marks are a guide as to how much you should write in your answers.

1 What is the day like on which the author sees his first peregrine? (3)

2 How does the author show that the other birds are uneasy about something? (6)

3 How does the author make the first sighting of the peregrine vivid and memorable? Use quotations to support your arguments. (6)

4 Explain the advice the author gives on how to approach peregrines. (6)

5 What impression do you have of the author? Explain your ideas with close reference to the text. (4)

Level 1

Read the passage entitled 'My First Peregrine', which is taken from *The Peregrine* by J. A. Baker, and then answer the following questions using complete sentences. The marks are a guide as to how much you should write in your answers.

1 Find two quotations that tell you it is a cold, wintry day on which the author sees his first peregrine. (2)

2 Alliteration is repeating consonant sounds in words that are close together and onomatopoeia is when a word sounds like what it is describing.

    (a) Look at lines 7–12. Write down one example of onomatopoeia and one of alliteration taken from these lines. (2)

    (b) Explain why you think the author might have used these here. (4)

3 Look at lines 20–26. The author is amazed by his encounter with the peregrine falcon.

    (a) Find two quotations that show this. (2)

    (b) Explain your choices. (4)

4 Look at lines 27–35.

    (a) In your own words write down three bits of advice the author gives on how to approach peregrines. (3)

    (b) Explain why you think this is good advice. (3)

5 If you had been with the author on the day he saw his first peregrine, would you have been as excited as he? Explain your point of view, using the text where appropriate. (5)

Paper 1, Section B: Writing task

Both levels

Write on any ONE of the following topics. Each one is worth 25 marks.

Credit will be given for good spelling, punctuation and presentation as well as for appropriate use of style and vocabulary.

1 You have been asked to write a short article to persuade people from your area to come to the school's open day.

2 Have you ever had to wait for an extremely long time, much longer than you thought? Write about your experience and what you did to help pass the time. Try to make the reader share your feelings.

3 Write a speech to be delivered to your class highlighting the positive and negative aspects of online computer games. Make sure you also give your own opinion.

4 EITHER

   (a) Books with happy endings are boring.

   Have you found this to be true? Discuss the statement using your own reading to support your arguments.

   OR

   (b) For a story to be interesting there must be some form of attachment between the two main characters.

   By referring to your own reading, explain how a relationship between the two main characters can make a story more enjoyable.

Cynddylan on a Tractor

Ah, you should see Cynddylan on a tractor.
Gone the old look that yoked him to the soil;
He's a new man now, part of the machine,
His nerves of metal and his blood oil.
5 The clutch curses, but the gears obey
His least bidding, and lo, he's away
Out of the farmyard, scattering hens.
Riding to work now as a great man should,
He is the knight at arms breaking the fields'
10 Mirror of silence, emptying the wood
Of foxes and squirrels and bright jays.
The sun comes over the tall trees
Kindling all the hedges, but not for him
Who runs his engine on a different fuel.
15 And all the birds are singing, bills wide in vain,
As Cynddylan passes proudly up the lane.

R.S. Thomas

Level 2

Read the poem 'Cynddylan on a Tractor' written by Welsh poet R. S. Thomas and published in 1952 and then answer the following questions using complete sentences. The marks are a guide as to how much you should write in your answers.

1 Why do you think the poem starts with 'Ah'? (2)

2 How does the poet bring across the novelty of Cynddylan on a tractor? You should use short quotations from the poem in your answer. (8)

3 What do we learn about Cynddylan from the poem? Use quotations to support your arguments. (6)

4 What does the poem suggest about the relationship of technology, man and nature? Explain your thoughts carefully, using words from the poem where appropriate. (4)

5 The end of Thomas's poem refers to the birds singing 'in vain'. Imagine you are a bird. Write a short piece describing what you might think about Cynddylan, using the poem to guide you. (5)

Level 1

Read the poem 'Cynddylan on a Tractor' written by Welsh poet R. S. Thomas, published in 1952, and then answer the following questions using complete sentences. The marks are a guide as to how much you should write in your answers.

1 What has happened to Cynddylan in the poem? (2)

2 Look at lines 3–9.
   (a) Write down two quotations which create a vivid picture of Cynddylan on the tractor. (2)
   (b) Explain what each quotation tells you about Cynddylan. (4)

3 Look at lines 6–15.
   How does nature react to Cynddylan? (6)

4 Look at the whole poem. The tractor could be a blessing or a curse.
   (a) Write down one quotation which suggests the tractor is a good thing and one which suggests the opposite. (2)
   (b) Explain what each quotation tells us about the tractor and how it helps or hinders man. (4)

5 Line 16 tells us that Cynddylan 'passes proudly' up the lane. Would you be proud if you were in his shoes? Use quotations to support your ideas, where appropriate. (5)

Paper 2, Section B: Writing task

Both levels

Write on any ONE of the following topics. Each one is worth 25 marks.

Credit will be given for good spelling, punctuation and presentation as well as for imaginative and exciting use of vocabulary.

1 The Mirror.

2 'You'll never grow up'
   Write a story that includes this sentence.

3 Write a story or description using one of the following titles:
   Learning the Hard Way
   The Stream
   If Only It Had Been Me

4 Taking a Risk.

Appendix

Planning sheets

These planning sheets are included to give you an idea of how to plan. For this reason there is a sample plan included after each template. You may also choose to photocopy the blank sheets to use for practice, but remember that you are not allowed to take any materials that might help you into the exam itself.

Plan for writing to persuade or argue

Title: _____

Pro	Con

Conclusion:

Order of points:

Persuasive	Discursive
Start with strongest, getting weaker	All points from one side
Sandwich counter arguments in own points	All points from other side
Repeat two strongest at end	Conclusion

Sample plan for writing to ~~persuade~~ ~~or~~ argue

Title: Every child should learn to play a musical instrument.

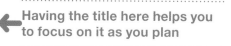 Having the title here helps you to focus on it as you plan

Pro	Con
1 It's creative and can help unlock artistic or creative potential	1 Not everyone has talent for music
2 It gives you pleasure	2 Reading music is an additional – complex – skill that pupils need to learn when many can't read words properly
3 It sounds good (once you can play)	3 Games is a sufficient counterbalance to academic lessons
4 It deepens appreciation for music	4 Learning a musical instrument is hard work and by making everyone learn one you are setting pupils up to be frustrated
5 There's too much emphasis on academics and it's a good counterbalance to sitting at a desk	5 It sounds awful when you are practising

Conclusion:

While playing of musical instruments should be encouraged, it's clearly not for everyone. Perhaps have option on some days between music and games.

Order of points:

Pro – 1, 2, 4, 5, 3

Con – 5, 4, 1, 2, 3

← You can, of course, change the number in your pros and cons table rather than write out the order again.

Plan for writing to explain, advise or inform

Title: _____

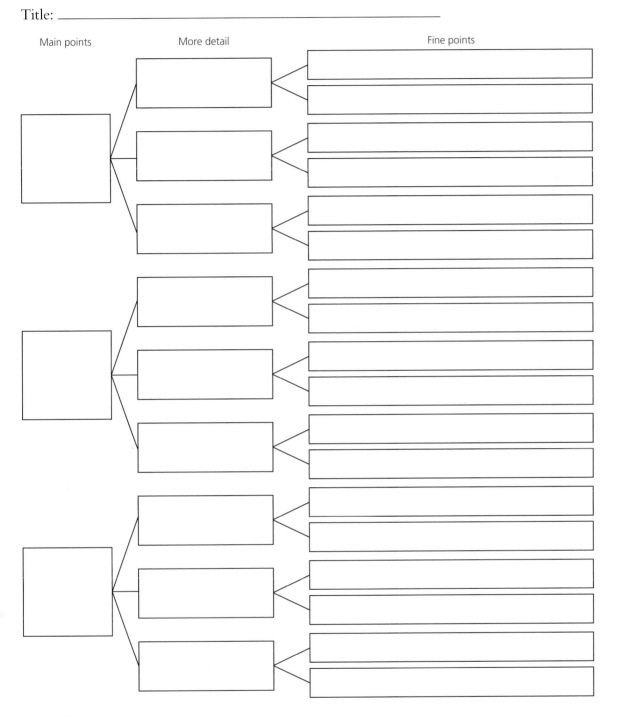

Main points   More detail   Fine points

Conclusion:

Explain	Advise	Inform
Make main points again	Give own opinion	State where further information is available

Sample plan for writing to explain
~~advise or inform~~

Title: Explain what a typical school day looks like.

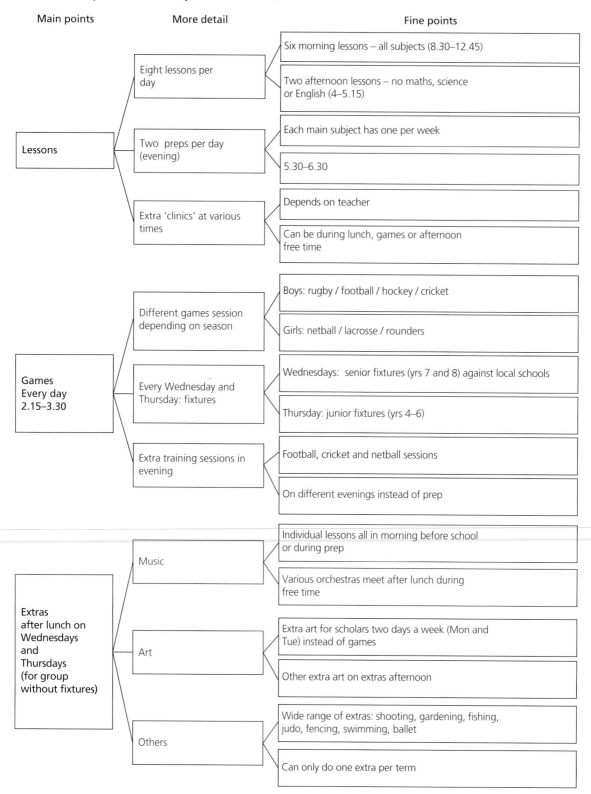

Main points	More detail	Fine points

Lessons

Eight lessons per day
- Six morning lessons – all subjects (8.30–12.45)
- Two afternoon lessons – no maths, science or English (4–5.15)

Two preps per day (evening)
- Each main subject has one per week
- 5.30–6.30

Extra 'clinics' at various times
- Depends on teacher
- Can be during lunch, games or afternoon free time

Games
Every day
2.15–3.30

Different games session depending on season
- Boys: rugby / football / hockey / cricket
- Girls: netball / lacrosse / rounders

Every Wednesday and Thursday: fixtures
- Wednesdays: senior fixtures (yrs 7 and 8) against local schools
- Thursday: junior fixtures (yrs 4–6)

Extra training sessions in evening
- Football, cricket and netball sessions
- On different evenings instead of prep

Extras
after lunch on Wednesdays and Thursdays (for group without fixtures)

Music
- Individual lessons all in morning before school or during prep
- Various orchestras meet after lunch during free time

Art
- Extra art for scholars two days a week (Mon and Tue) instead of games
- Other extra art on extras afternoon

Others
- Wide range of extras: shooting, gardening, fishing, judo, fencing, swimming, ballet
- Can only do one extra per term

Conclusion:

Compare time for lessons (4hr + 1), games (1hr 15) and extras (1hr) per day.

Plan for writing about a book

Title: _____

	Scene 1	Scene 2	Scene 3
Summary			
Answer to title			
Why scenes similar/different			

↓ ↓ ↓

Conclusion

Sample plan for writing about a book

Title: Reading tells you more about the world. Do you agree?

	Scene 1	Scene 2	Scene 3
Summary	Macbeth – Lady M persuades M to kill Duncan by calling him a coward	Macbeth – Macbeth killed by Macduff in battle	Harry Potter – Harry discovers he's a wizard
Answer to title	Yes: find out how people manipulate each other to achieve goals, how weak men can be Lady Macbeth is scheming and plots carefully to get M to do her bidding	No: Straightforward battle. Not a lot to learn. M gains courage again and fights fate, but nothing really new about world	No: As this is fantasy it doesn't tell me anything about world. No process which can be related to real world
Why scenes similar/different	Yes because there is insight into characters and how they manipulate	No because straightforward scene in which little character development. It's just a battle and as such nothing new	No because it is fantasy and no scene that develops character

$$\downarrow \qquad\qquad \downarrow \qquad\qquad \downarrow$$

Conclusion
Scenes show that we learn new things if there is character development; learn how people act. If fantasy or everyday occurrence with no character development, we tend not to learn.

Glossary

The following includes the main techniques you may come across or need to explain in your Common Entrance exam. Terms that have been introduced in this guide are also covered. Entries with an asterisk (★) are techniques specifically mentioned in the ISEB syllabus as ones you should know for poetry comprehensions.

★Alliteration The repetition of the same consonant sound in several words that are close together. The consonants do not all have to be at the beginning of the words and the words do not have to be one after the other. Alliteration with an 's' sound is called **sibilance**.

Alliteration helps stress the sound of a scene. In some ways it is therefore similar to **onomatopoeia**, and is related to **assonance**.

e.g. The cla**tt**er and ra**tt**le of the **t**in-**t**opped box

(The repetition of the short, sharp 't' sound matches metal being hit or striking repeatedly, which is what happens when it clatters and rattles.)

Analogy The illustration of a more complicated idea by comparison with a more simple idea that resembles it in its main points. An analogy can be a short image or a more extended comparison of images to illustrate an idea. It is often an extended **simile**.

e.g. His heart was like an old grandfather clock that had been wound up one last time and was now inexorably winding down, the pendulum slowing with each sweep.

Anapaest A metrical **foot**. An anapaest consists of three syllables, of which the third is stressed. Anapaests are usually mixed with **iambs**; pure lines of anapaests are rare in English **poetry**.

e.g. croc-o-DILE

e.g. I will TELL | you a TALE | of a VE- | ry small BOY

(This is a line of anapaestic tetrameter, as it contains four anapaests.)

Anecdote A little story, usually humorous, about real events. Anecdotes often liven up non-fiction writing or conversation. They often begin with 'The best thing was ...' or 'It was so funny when ...' or similar introductory remarks.

Antagonist The opponent of the **protagonist**. The antagonist is more familiarly known as the 'baddie' (if the main character is the 'goodie', that is). As such, the antagonist opposes the **hero or heroine** and makes life for him or her difficult and is often only vanquished at the very end. If the hero is evil (as in *Macbeth*), then the antagonist will necessarily be good.

★Assonance The repetition of the same vowel sound in several words that are close together. The vowels do not all have to be spelt the same and the words do not have to be one after the other.

Assonance helps stress the sound of a scene. In some ways it is therefore similar to **onomatopoeia** and is related to **alliteration**.

e.g. The m**ee**k shall rec**ei**ve eternal p**ea**ce.

(The repetition of the long 'ee' sound creates an atmosphere of rest and calm, which matches the statement.)

Autobiography The non-fiction account of (a part of) the life of a person, written by that person. If the life story is written by someone else, it is a **biography**.

Bias Looking at an issue or person with a prejudiced, pre-formed positive or negative opinion; writing about something in a one-sided way.

Biography The non-fiction account of (a part of) the life of a person, written by someone other than that person. If the life story is written by that person, it is an **autobiography**.

Blank verse Lines of **iambic** pentameter that do not rhyme. In English **poetry** blank verse is the standard form for heroic or dramatic verse. John Milton's *Paradise Lost* as well as most of Shakespeare's verse is in blank verse.

e.g. (from Milton's *Paradise Lost*)

Of MAN'S | first DIS- | o-BE- | dience AND | the FRUIT

Of THAT | for-BI- | dden TREE |whose MOR- | tal TASTE ...

Do not confuse this with **free verse**.

Chiasmus A literary technique based around the letter 'X' (*chi* in Greek). It involves mirroring (or crossing) the words of one clause into the following, parallel clause. The words don't actually have to be the same, but must correspond in some way.

e.g. She's hated if clever; if stupid, despised.

(The mirror is at the semicolon: 'clever' and 'stupid' correspond, as do 'hated' and 'despised'. If the clauses are written underneath one another, the construction becomes clear:

She's hated if clever;

if stupid, despised)

Colloquial language Everyday informal language. This is the way most people talk. Colloquial language is often used in **dialogue** to add realism or to show a character's character. It should not be used in formal writing.

e.g. ''Ow's 'ee ta know?'

   Mercutio and Tybalt beat each other up.

Consonance The use of a number of words that have the same consonants in the stressed syllable.

e.g. The s**p**ee**d** of s**p**a**d**es

Consonant or consonantal rhyme The use of consonance at the end of lines of **poetry** as a more modern form of **rhyme**.

e.g. (from Wilfred Owen's 'Strange Meeting')

It seemed that out of battle I escaped
Down some profound dull tunnel, long since scooped
Through granites which titanic wars had groined.
Yet also there encumbered sleepers groaned ...

Context The surroundings of (part of) a text that helps to clarify its meaning. This can be the text or punctuation immediately before and after a certain extract as well as the circumstances or the time in which the text was written.

e.g. Depending on context, 'That's great!' can be an expression of joy or of disappointment; the words alone are insufficient to convey the intended meaning.

Couplet In **poetry** two lines (usually of the same metre) that **rhyme**. They do not have to be able to stand alone, but often do.

e.g.

What is it in a baby's drool
That all around must play the fool?

Dactyl A metrical **foot**. A dactyl consists of three syllables, of which the first is stressed. Dactyls are usually mixed with **trochees**; pure lines of dactyls are rare in English **poetry**.

e.g. BEAU-ti-ful
   DAN-ger-ous | PEO-ple, ac- | CEPT this gift

(This is a line of dactylic trimeter, as it contains three dactyls.)

Descriptive language Words used in such a way as to represent as complete a feel for a situation as possible, making the reader feel as though she or he were actually there.

Deus ex machina A surprising, because completely unforeseeable, and usually illogical, sudden happy end to a seemingly hopeless situation. The arrival of the eagles at the end of both Tolkien's *The Hobbit* and *The Lord of the Rings* is a deus ex machina.

Dialogue Direct speech between two or more characters. It is one of the main techniques in drama and is used heavily in **prose** fiction, but usually less in **poetry**.

Dramatic irony When the audience knows more than the character in the story does. Usually, the audience knows that a character's expectations will not be fulfilled, and therefore understands the words of that character differently from how they are intended.

e.g. When Bottom, as a donkey, in *A Midsummer Night's Dream*, states 'I see their knavery. This is to make an ass of me', Shakespeare is using dramatic irony, because the audience knows that Bottom has in fact become an ass, while he is blissfully unaware. The audience therefore understands Bottom's words differently from him.

Ellipsis A punctuation mark [...] used to show that words have been left out.

Ellipsis is also leaving out words that are necessary to understand a statement completely, but which can be guessed from the **context**. This technique is often used in modern poetry as well as by pupils.

e.g. 'It's like, you know ... like.'

(This quotation uses two forms of ellipses. Whether the missing words can actually be guessed from the context will depend very much on the context.)

e.g. I will to Mantua.

(The word 'go' has been left out, but it is clear from the context that this is what is meant.)

Enjambment When the meaning of a line of **poetry** runs into the next line. Although this technique has been widely used since Shakespeare's time, most pupils are under the impression that there must be a pause at the end of a line and therefore read to the end of a line rather than to a punctuation mark and thus miss the enjambment as well as the meaning of the lines.

e.g.

When I next meet
Him I shall greet
Him and say,
'Have a good day!'

(Here the first three lines are enjambed and only lines three and four are end-stopped. If a reader were to pause at the end of either line one or two, the text would not make any sense.)

Euphemism Using a positive sounding word or phrase instead of a rude or negative word or phrase.

e.g. 'crossing over' instead of 'dying'

Feminine rhyme A form of **rhyme** in which the rhyming stressed syllable is followed by another unstressed syllable, which must have the same sound in each case.
e.g. (the stressed syllables are in capitals)

If only I could find or BO-rrow
Some comfort to undo your SO-rrow

(The words 'borrow' and 'sorrow' form a feminine rhyme.)

Flashback A jump into the past. Flashbacks or retrospectives are scenes that are prior to the time of the story, but are inserted into the flow of the story. Flashbacks therefore relate events that happened before the story began and break up the time sequence of the story.

Foot In **poetry** the name given to the smallest unit of **rhythm**. The number and kind of feet in a line make up the **metre** of a poem.

Fragment An unfinished piece of writing. This can be on purpose or accidental.

Free verse A type of **poetry** that is irregular in that it does not have a set **rhyme scheme** (if it uses rhyme at all) or a fixed **metre**. A large number of modern poems are written in free verse.

Genre Types of stories or writing. Genre is a category of story that follows certain rules and conventions, which make it recognisable (e.g. a ghost story will always have some element of the supernatural in it).

Examples of genre are:

fantasy, science-fiction, autobiography, journalism, memoirs, historical fiction, travel writing, poetry, tragedy.

Half-rhyme Two words that do not quite **rhyme**, due to the vowel sounds being slightly different (although the same vowel) or the consonants of the stressed syllable not quite matching. In many ways, a half-rhyme can be regarded as a **consonant rhyme**.

e.g.

walk – talked (Because 'talked' has the unstressed syllable '-ed' at the end, it is not a pure rhyme.)

fight – lights (The 's' at the end of 'lights' makes this a half-rhyme.)

fool – full (The two words almost rhyme, but the 'u' sound in both words is not quite the same, making it a half-rhyme.)

Hero or heroine The main character in a story, the person that the story is about. In a first-person narrative the hero is also the narrator. A hero does not have to have any heroic qualities (like fighting dragons, being virtuous and courageous or flying through the sky).

Hyperbole Another word for exaggeration. This literary technique is often used for comic effect or to persuade people of one's own opinion (because the other is too horrific to entertain).

e.g. If you abolish the monarchy, Britain will slip back into the Stone Age.

Iamb A **foot** or metrical unit of **poetry** that consists of two syllables of which the second is stressed (i.e. ti-TUM).

Iambic metre is by far the most commonly used form of **metre** in English poetry.

e.g. re-SULT, ca-NOE, e-VENT

Imagery Using pictures, smells, sounds, taste or texture in words to describe a person, object, experience or feeling. While this can be done through simple words, imagery is usually conveyed by **simile** or **metaphor**.

e.g. A squall blew the rain across the marshes. (simple language)
The mist clung to my coat with clammy hands. (metaphor)
The heat of the sun was as oppressive as a hammer pounding metal thin on an anvil. (simile)

Internal rhyme When words **rhyme** within lines rather than at the end of lines. Internal rhymes can be within one line or between two lines.

e.g.

The wind lay stale against the sail in the motionless blue.

Like waves her hair across the ocean curls;

On currents warm past pearls and corals ...

Inversion A reversal of position or order. The term is usually applied to a change in word order to emphasise certain words. Yoda in *The Empire Strikes Back* makes frequent use of inversions, not to stress words, but because he cannot speak proper English.

e.g. Loudly shout your rage to the skies!

(The adverb should be after the verb, but is placed before it here, to emphasise it.)

Through the streets raced the rat.

(The normal word order has been inverted to emphasise the subject of the sentence.)

★Irony Meaning one thing, but saying the exact opposite, usually to achieve a humorous effect. To be understood, irony relies heavily on **context**.

Masculine rhyme A form of **rhyme** in which the stressed syllables at the end of lines rhyme.

e.g. (the stressed syllables are in capitals)

When ghosts beat darkly on the PANE

And moonlight boils in blood a-GAIN ...

(The words 'pane' and 'again' form a masculine rhyme.)

★Metaphor An image. A thing or action is referred to using a picture or words that normally apply to a different object or action, which has something in common with the first thing or action. We use many metaphors in our everyday speech (probably without realising it), e.g. he's a pig, she hit the nail on the head. In literature, especially **poetry**, metaphors are more adventurous than this and thrive on the unexpectedness, but aptness, of the image.

e.g.

The ragged edges of the wounds that bite
With new-found teeth ...

(While the wound may well have ragged edges, it cannot bite. The verb metaphorically refers to the pain the wound causes. Similarly, the wound has no teeth; this is a metaphor for 'the ragged edges' that hurt the skin much as though they were inwardly turned teeth.)

*Metre The formal and regular **rhythm** of a line of **poetry**. In English, metre is based on a mixture of stressed and unstressed syllables. Metre is made up of a number of feet. It is important to understand that metric **feet** do not need to match the words, but can span or split words. Depending on how many feet a line has, we talk of different kinds of lines, such as tetrameter and pentameter (four and five feet per line respectively), to name only the most common ones. The most frequently used metres in English are **iambic** pentameter and iambic tetrameter. However, **trochaic**, **dactylic** and **anapaestic** metre are also possible, although the latter two are rarely used in a pure form.

e.g. (stressed syllables are capitalised)

And DID | those FEET | in AN- | cient TIME ...

(William Blake – iambic tetrameter)

BRI-ttle | GRASS cut | THROUGH his | SKIN as | CAU-tious- | LY he ...

(trochaic hexameter)

COME to my | ARMS little | CHILD of mine

(dactylic trimeter)

The a-SSY- | rian came DOWN | like the WOLF | on the FOLD ...

(Lord Byron – anapaestic tetrameter)

Onomatopoeia A literary technique that uses words to mirror the sound they describe.

e.g. sizzle

The wild wind whistled through the spinney.

(The word 'whistled' is onomatopoeic as it resembles the sound it describes. The **alliteration** with the 'w' sound strengthens this effect, making the whole sentence sound like the wind.)

Oxymoron Combining two opposite concepts in a description.

e.g. darkness visible

(John Milton – darkness denies the sense of sight, so cannot be visible; Milton uses the oxymoron to emphasise that the darkness was so deep and tangible it could almost be seen.)

the damp fire of his desire

(Damp suggests wet, making it the opposite of fire; the oxymoron suggests that although his desire is strong and uncontrolled, he does not have the strength to act on it – it is damp, ineffective and soppy.)

Paragraph The start of a new line, often combined with an indentation. Paragraphs are used:

- to highlight direct speech and when there is a switch of person talking
- when there is a change in subject matter
- for new lines of **poetry**
- for lists
- for emphasis or effect.

Pathetic fallacy Giving the natural world feelings, usually to reflect a certain mood in the story.

e.g. The wind howled in rage, rattled at shutters and slammed doors in unbridled fury.

*Personification A figure of speech that gives human characteristics to non-humans or refers to non-humans as though they were human.

e.g. Joy took Time by the hands and together they danced and leapt in the grass.

This – classical – form of personification is hardly used anymore. Personification for most is now nothing more than a 'humanised' **metaphor**. I would argue that it can only be personification if the endowment with human characteristics is prolonged.

Thus:

The sun tickled me awake.

(This is a metaphor, although the sun is carrying out a human activity.)

The sun raised its head from its pillow of clouds and looked at the grey sky. Reluctantly, it got up, dragged itself to the shower and made itself ready for the work ahead, although it would have preferred to spend the overcast day in bed.

(This is personification, as the sun is being treated as a human for an extended time.)

Pleonasm Using more words than are necessary to convey the meaning.

e.g. He ran with his feet moving quickly.

Poem, poetry An intense and condensed form of writing organised into lines and usually based on some form of **rhythm**. A good poem is a combination of unusual and intense language and fresh thought, no matter whether the content is serious or comical. Poetry usually makes frequent use of **imagery** and other literary techniques to involve the audience directly.

It is well worth reading what various people (in particular poets) at various times have thought defines poetry, as there is no agreed definition. **Rhymes** in birthday cards and the like are definitely *not* poetry, but verse.

Prose Ordinary writing. Writing organised into sentences and **paragraphs**, without a rhythmical pattern and without condensed language.

Protagonist Another name for the **hero or heroine** of a story.

Proverb A generally well-known saying that very briefly states received wisdom.

e.g. A bird in the hand is worth two in the bush.

   A stitch in time saves nine.

Repetition Saying a word or a phrase again, usually for emphasis. Sometimes, repetition is used instead of **rhyme** for some lines of a poem.

e.g. **We must all** hold together, **we must all** join hands to stand strong, **we must all** share one vision if we are to change the world.

(Here repetition is used for emphasis.)

e.g.

We looked up at the **sun**
To see the works not done
How the sky engulfed our hopes
Burnt our dreams
To flecks of rust on the **sun**.

(Lines one and two and two and five rhyme, but lines one and five do not rhyme; the last word is merely repeated.)

Rhetorical question A question that is used to persuade rather than to receive an answer; the answer is often simple, known and too obvious to be given.

e.g. Who doesn't want to be happy?

★Rhyme The repetition of the sound of a stressed syllable, usually at the end of a line of **poetry**.

e.g.

dog – log (masculine rhyme)

utter – gutter (feminine rhyme)

crocodile – clock and dial (triple rhyme)

Rhyme scheme How rhymes are arranged in a poem. To be able to describe and talk about a rhyme scheme, a word is assigned a letter and any word that rhymes with it is given the same letter. Words that don't rhyme are given further letters.

e.g.

A limerick has the rhyme scheme a-a-b-b-a.

The following lines have the rhyme scheme a-b-a-c-d:

The green and purple hawkmoth loves the light
That effervesces from its sequined wings,
Collects in bulbs and reels, a satellite
Around the lunar constant of its self
Caught somewhere deep in outer space.

★Rhythm A pattern of stresses (beats) used most prominently and purposefully in **poetry**. Simply put, rhythm is measured in the number of stresses per line. Rhythm was born of the heartbeat (which is why poetry is more direct than **prose**) and is fundamental to life, the universe and everything.

Setting The reality in which a story takes place: its location and time. The setting is usually made clear in the first few sentences or **paragraphs** of a story.

Sibilance Is **alliteration** with the 's' sound. The repetition of the hissing 's' sound in words that are close together.

e.g. Swiftly and silently the ships slid into the black waves of the sea.

★Simile A comparison. A thing or action is compared to a different object or action, which has something in common with the first thing or action, using 'like' or 'as'. We use many similes in our everyday speech, e.g. she's as blind as a bat. Similes are common both in **prose** and **poetry**.

e.g. nostrils widen like the air intakes of fighter planes

Stanza Any division of a **poem** into shorter parts. Stanzas are usually regular (i.e. they have the same number of lines, **rhyme scheme** and **metre**), and thus form a pattern and give the poem structure. They are separated from each other by a line left blank.

Stream of consciousness A type of writing that copies the way someone thinks, remembers and feels, following the flow and jumps of associations and visions the brain makes. It is thinking, memory and feeling written down. In its pure form it often breaks the rules of grammar and punctuation, just as thoughts and feelings seldom come in sentences.

*****Symbol** A type of **imagery**, where a word references an object or action which has some deeper but unspecified meaning. While a **metaphor** is determined, a symbol is not and it is up to the reader to imbue the symbol with significance.

e.g. A mountain can be a symbol for a goal, for striving for something higher, for detachment

from the world, for something immovable as well as insurmountable difficulties – or a number of these at the same time.

Tautology (Unnecessarily) repeating the same thing twice, but in different words. Using synonyms to say the same thing.

e.g. He hit and beat her.

Theme The abstract subject matter of a text; the ideas and concepts a work deals with, such as betrayal, salvation or forgiveness.

Tricolon A pattern of three words, phrases or clauses.

e.g.

It was so cold, she put on a jumper, a hoodie and a coat.

The teacher would like you to stop what you are doing, face the front and pay attention.

veni vidi vici (C.I. Caesar)

Trochee A **foot** or metrical unit of **poetry** that consists of two syllables of which the first is stressed (i.e. TUM-ti).

e.g. WIN-dow, NA-nny, FA-ther

(All examples that are not credited are the author's.)